FOREST, FOLKS & FAMILY POEMS
Ashdown Forest & Elsewhere

Rosalie Leng

Pitcairn-Knowles Publishing
Sevenoaks

This book is sold subject to the condition that it shall not, by way of trade or otherwise, be hired out, photographed or held in any retrieval system or otherwise circulated without the publishers prior consent in any form of binding or cover other than that in which this is published and without a similar condition including this condition being imposed on the subsequent purchaser.

PKP
Pitcairn-Knowles Publishing
Springbank House
13 Pembroke Road
Sevenoaks Kent TN13 1XR
01959-523154
rppk@btinternet.com

First Published 2018
© Rosalie Leng

ISBN 978-0-9558591-7-5

A catalogue record for this book is available from
The British Library

Printed in Great Britain by:
ImpressionIT
Unit 2 Maunsell Road
St Leonards-on-Sea
East Sussex TN38 9NL
01424-852116

CONTENTS

Dedication			ix
Foreword:	Rosalie Leng		x
Introduction:	Richard Pitcairn-Knowles		xi
	How It All Started		xv

1. – Rosalie's Ashdown Forest News Poems

Autumnal Joy	2012	1
Mist Jewels	2012	2
Just Spring	2013	3
Fire and Ice	2013	4
A Forest Summer's Day	2014	6
Wrinkly Ramblers Walk Tall	2014	7
The Vachery in Spring	2015	8
Magical Illusions	2015	9
The Four Legged Forest Conservators	2016	10
Hip, Hip for the Haw	2016	12
A Walk-Camp Hill-Ellison's Pond	2017	13
Rest and Renewal	2017	14
A Prickly Matter for Pooh	2018	15
Friends' Clump	2018	16

2. – Rosalie's other poems

Rhymer in Residence	19
May Blossoms	20
Enter New Age – Exit in Rage	21
My 80th – Feb 2010	22
They Came for Tea	23
Mystic Masseur	24
Doves	24
Fun at Eighty-one	25
Sue at East Dean	26

Clyde House School	26
Winter Lingers Long	27
View Through the Window	28
Spring 2012	29
An Ode to Odious Weather	30
Awash - Drowning not Waving	31
The Holy Spider	32
Winter 2015/16	33
A Springtime Walk	34
The High and Mighty Bed	35
Have Some Madeira M'Dear	37
The Tale of the Madeira Tout	38
The Weary Walkers Wail	39
Transient Spring	39
The Happy Wanderers	40
High Weald Waddlers	40
Whacky Weird Walkers are We	41
A Walker's Warning	42
A Talkers Warning	43
Kushti's Last Summers 2002-2003	44

3 – Irene Case - Rosalie's Mother's Poetry

Untitled	45
The Nightmare	45
Fear Hath Torment	48
Gone	48
To David	49
The Scourge	49
The Slug	49
Abracadabra	50
Dreams	50
Another Dream	50
An Allegory	51
A Gardener's Lament	51

The Baker – for David	52
A Wish	52
To David	53
Cats	53
Dogs	54
Golden Retriever	54
Flowers	54
To my Valentine	55
1956 – When her husband retired	55
Convalescence 1973	56
To Bill – A Floral Border	56
Ivan	57
A Song to Ivan	57
Rabbits	57
Sunset	58
Autumn	58
Grandad	58
Fiji (The poodle)	58
Memory	59
Dalmation	59
Kate and Meg	60
A Poem	60
The Pine Wood	61
The Ever Changing Sea	63
The Sun	65

4 - Rosalie's Grandsons' Poems

Crispin Dear Nana – Happy Birthday	67
April '01	67
Twenty Meters of Land	68
Crispin's Poem August 2001	68
The Biggest Lie	69
Nana's House	70
To Our Darling Nana	71

For Gintare 2018	71
The Land of Shadows	72
Leeds United's Title Dream	73
Marvin Midnight Breeze	74
A Tribute to Amy	74
Alex A Sea of Blood	75

5 - Tributes to others from Rosalie

Binoculars	77
A Birthday Limerick	78
Tribute to Pat James	79
To Poppy	81
For Stephanie	81
To Tamsin and Lindsay	82
If	82
You Came, We Saw, You Conquered 2011	83
Marvin	83
Crispin for his 9th Birthday	84
Una Wareham's 61st	84
To David, the Loving Gardener	85
So Wise!	86
Our Visit to Family in California	87
You Gotta Have a Dream	88
The Sad Tale of Maisie's Lost Tail	88
Action Stations	89
To Eileen	90
Irene and John Go West	91
Eccentricity	92
A Tribute to Pamela who died 5.2.96	93
A Letter to Wendy	94
To Wendy on her 70th Birthday	95
Agile & Mobile with Style 2010 For Alan	96
Keith	97

Sonia's 60th Birthday	98
To My Good Friend Sue	98
To Sue 1997	99
In Memory of Mick Sep 2008	99
To Flora and the Ladies who Sew	100
For Stephanie's 60th Birthday	101
A Day With Eileen	101
56th Anniversary	102
Jean's 60th Birthday '92	102
1996 Visit to Belgium	103
Tamsin on her 12th Birthday	104
For Kali	104
Dianne	105
Pearl Wedding 60th & 65th Birthdays Larry & Ann	106
Tamsin & Lindsay	106
Crispin	107
To Nicholas on his 35th Birthday Oct '92	108
Fond Farewell to Ivan and Family Oct '94	109
A Thankyou to Sue Watts	110
Sue Again '95	111
To Ronnie on his 63rd Birthday	112
Flora's Birthday	113
Love's Labours Won – April 2015	113
Nigel	114
Sonia & Nigel's Golden Anniversary 2004	115
To Pat	116
Apologies to Lewis Carroll 1986	117
Suzie's 30th Birthday May 1992	118
Bit of Blarney for Barnie, Belle of the Ball	119
Another Bit of Blarney for Barnie, Xmas	120
To Irene 1980	121
Holidays at Triton for Marvin	122

ILLUSTRATIONS

	Page
The Leng Family in 2013	ix
The Gang	xii
David, Rosalie & Richard	xiii
Mist Jewels	2
Fire and Ice	5
Forest Conservators	11
A Prickly Matter for Pooh Bear	15
Friends' Clump	17
Thanks to Rosalie	18
Irene Case (neé Davies) Rosalie's Mother	46
William Case Rosalie's Father	47
Rosalie and Ronnie's Grandsons	66
The Alphabet by Irene	76
The Boys and Rosalie on holiday	123
The Leng Family in 1993	126

Front Cover Photo: Camp Hill by Rosalie Leng
Back Cover Photos: By Gintare & Rosalie Leng

DEDICATION

I would like to dedicate this book to my dearest husband who has encouraged me, my sons, my five grandsons and my great-grandchildren who have all given me so much happiness in my life, with the hope that they will remember our adventures and fun on Ashdown Forest and laugh a little at my nonsense.

The Leng Family in 2013
Jeremy, Nick, Midori, Ivan, Alex,
Kali, Mollie, Crispin, Rosalie, Ronnie, Susie, Julie,
Frey, Marvin, Oliver.

FOREWORD
Rosalie Leng

This little book of mine and my family's rhymes was born from a wish to pass on some very happy memories to my grandchildren and their children.

But it would have remained a 'twinkle in my eye' and never been born if it hadn't been for my childhood friend, Richard Pitcairn-Knowles. It was his suggestion, his knowledge of publishing and enthusiastic support which literally (full meaning) made my idea materialise into print, which little book will, hopefully, give amusement and enjoyment to my family and friends – and possibly others.

There are a few poems from my grandchildren, written during summer holidays, and many short, imaginative poems from my mother, Irene Case, who had a very perceptive wit and understanding of human weaknesses and depth of feeling – and there are a couple from her sister, Ida. Of course, there are a lot of mine; I think some of the best ones are about Ashdown forest. Many were written for friends and some zany, nonsensical ones (quality rather lacking!) were especially written to amuse our grandsons and to remind them of the great fun we had together in school holidays.

Again, I would like to thank Richard, from the bottom of my heart, for making a dream come true.

INTRODUCTION
Richard Pitcairn-Knowles

For many years Rosalie Leng has contributed articles and poems to many magazines, and been an active member of the Tunbridge Wells Writers Group. She also names Ashdown Forest and Lord Byron as her inspirations, especially this extract from Byron's 'Childe Harold's Pilgrimage'

> *There is a pleasure in the pathless woods,*
> *There is rapture on the lonely shore,*
> *There is society, where none intrudes,*
> *By the deep sea and music in its roar;*
> *I love not Man the less, but nature more,*
> *From these our interviews, in which I steal*
> *From all I may be, or have been before,*
> *To mingle with the Universe and I feel*
> *What I can ne'er express, yet cannot all conceal.*

Having persuaded Rosalie that her work could, and indeed should, be published to be enjoyed by a wider readership and, of course, closer to home, experienced by her descendants, I feel it is imperative to explain the tenuous connection she and I have had for the last eighty years. She is due grateful thanks, and I am delighted that she has allowed me to publish this collection of her poetry.

Rosalie (neé Case) was born in Haslemere in February 1930. When she was five the family moved to the characterfully rough, and never finished, Parkwood Road, off The Ridge, five hundred feet above, and on the edge of,

Hastings. They settled there to keep chickens commercially. As soon as possible Rosalie was off with the rest of the friendly 'gang' of local children and we played in the nearby woods and streams, her love of which is now transferred to the wide open spaces of Ashdown Forest.

Early in World War Two, when destruction came to Hastings, Rosalie had close up views of enemy fighter-bombers roaring over her home, at roof-top height, on their way to drop bombs on Hastings before sweeping back over The Channel to their bases in France. Later in the war when a V1 Doodlebug exploded in her beloved woods, no more than a

The Parkwood Road Gang, 1940

David (Rosalie's brother), Rosalie & Richard in Parkwood Road, Hastings enjoying the severe and drawn out winter from January to March in 1942 during WW2. The winter of 1941-1942 was the coldest European winter of the twentieth century.

76 years later! Rosalie & Richard, on the same toboggan at her home in Crowborough in the less cold January of 2018. Sadly, her brother, David, is not there; he died a few years before this. Photo by Ronnie Leng.

quarter of a mile away, the house was surprisingly undamaged, but that same Doodlebug shattered the windows at my home, Riposo Health Hydro. The 'gang' continued to play, in 'their' woods, untroubled by these events. As they grew older the children of the 'gang' went their separate ways and had mostly lost contact with each other by about 1946.

About forty years later Rosalie came across my name at Sevenoaks and phoned me! Over seventy years since we lost contact, we have now 'ganged up' once again to collect her lovely Ashdown Forest poems together, with others she has written over the years. Her grandchildren wrote poetry when young and she has carefully guarded the many poems written by her mother. Crispin continues to write lyrics for his music.

The purpose of this book is to bring this poetic gift, which runs through generations of her family, together in one volume for a wider readership to enjoy, especially her grandchildren. In this collection of family poems there is beauty, there is humour, there is fascination with this gift which this artistic family has unconsciously passed down from generation to generation.

Rosalie and her husband, Ronnie, have lived for many years in Crowborough, where they brought up their children on the edge of Ashdown Forest. Incidentally, Ronnie Leng was my hero when he broke the long jump record at Hastings Grammar School! When the 'gang' drifted apart, and Rosalie blossomed into a tall and elegantly attractive seventeen-year-old, she first met Ronnie, as described in her early poem, *'A Jingle-Jangle Dedication to my Ronnie'*. The early part of this poem was written soon after they first met and the later verses were added as the courtship moved on to marriage!

How It All Started
A Jingle-Jangle Dedication to my Ronnie

I played in the sea one fine June day
Then whom should I see not far away
But a handsome, blond young man
Wading towards me like Tarzan.

Shyly he came and sat quite near,
Said he was a cousin dear
Of Margaret Slater – whom I knew
As a friend of my friend's sister, Phew!
What a smart and devious ploy
Was used by this still teen-age boy!

Often I met him on the shore
And joined his good friends, boys all four.
Girls on the beach watched with envy
But he alone was the one I could see.

This went on for quite a while
To hurry things was not his style,
Then one day when on my own
He asked me out and changed his tone!

Glorious times we had together,
Swimming, boat trips in marvellous weather,
Walking to Fairlight, riding in lanes,
Trips in the car, and rides in planes.

October came, the sun began to wane,
We went to plays and pictures again.
Occasional dips in swim baths we took
But photography Ronnie never forsook!

We had music in plenty and enjoyments galore
Then Christmas was coming, and we foresaw
Two years in the RAF would seem very slow,
But hopefully speaking, they might quickly go.

He'll be back in February once more
"X equals a lemon" – that's Ronnie's law.
His "square-bashing" finished, my Woolly Bear
Will find his own Cherub awaiting him here!

LAC Leng will be due for demob
In no time at all he'll be seeking a job –
Lawyer, pen-pusher, farmer or pilot,
What he likes best – to guess, I cannot.

Ronnie completed his National Service and several years articled to an accountancy firm in Hastings and they were married in 1953 at Old Bradwell, in Buckinghamshire, by Rosalie's uncle, the Reverend Conway Davies. They first lived in a flat in London Road, St Leonards, before moving to Trinidad for six years where all three boys were born. As the children grew older the family moved back to England and have lived in Crowborough ever since.

1 - POEMS FOR ASHDOWN FOREST

<u>Autumnal Joy</u>
Autumn 2012

Joy ...
In leaves,
Whispering, fluttering,
Golden, shimmering,
Claret-red and bronze a-gleaming.

Feet a-rustling,
Wind, a-bustling,
Wafting, floating, earth a-coating
With dead leaves curling,
Blustering, whirling.

Boots, crackling, crunching
Through leaves, a-bunching
In wind-blown heaps
Our swinging feet sweeping
Leaves swirling, leaping,
As childhood we're keeping
Our joy ...
In leaves,
Whispering, fluttering,
Golden, shimmering,
Russet and bronze a-glimmering.

Mist Jewels
Spring 2013

Silver mist scatters stars in grass,
Stars, crushed by the feet which pass.
But the silk-spinner, wonder weaver,
Invisibly, her nets are spread
With patient skill – artful deceiver!

But now, bejewelled and diamond-dewed,
Gauzy webs shine, pearlized,
Each new design, with art so fine,
A fatal trap spun with thread ...
Sparkling,
Now so visible!
No longer an insect's dread,
Today, no swaddling of insects glued
In web bejewelled and diamond-dewed!
Just boots which pass o'er starry grass.

Mist Jewels – Spring 2013 - Photo by Richard Pitcairn-Knowles

Just Spring
Spring 2013

There's a cadence of Spring, sung … hesitantly,
Now – a flurry of feathers, an urgency,
The leaf-buds, rose-tipped, are uncurling,
Brimstone's sun-warmed wings unfurling.

So we'll walk the woods and tread with care
Through the bluebell lakes' translucent glimmer.
There windflowers sparkle in dappled light;
The birch leaves shake in a sunny shimmer,
And blackthorn is draped in skeins of white.

We'll walk the paths and pause, where, unaware,
Herds of deer, tails a-flicker, on new leaves graze.
Now the lordly beech is hazed in green,
The humble violet hiding from our gaze
In shady growth, seems shy to be seen.

Now on the heathy hills we'll stop and stare
Following the dot, up through opalescent haze,
To find the lark, ethereal spirit of the air
Singing its glorious ode in praise
Of things to be and have always been –
Spring.

So, I also give God thanks
For the promise of life renewing,
And the hope that is ensuing.
For … just Spring.

Fire and Ice
Autumn 2013

Berry bright ...
Rowan sparkles ruby fire
And blackbird strives for his desire.

Berry bright ...
Roseate hedgerows gleam and glow
And thorny branch holds purple sloe.
Its damson bloom draws my sight
On a sunny noon, but it leaves scars
On hands which have no right
To steal,
Its
Berries bright ...
In the Autumn light.

Frost bright ...
Diamond-sprinkled spikes of grass
Now fretted shards of ice like glass.

Frost bright ...
Mossy turf, star speckled white,
Now twinkling rime encrusts.
But walkers' feet crush stars to dust
On a chilly morn, to leave scars
Where only a fox trod, light,
In the frost,
Last
Frost bright ...
Moonlight night.

Fire and Ice – Autumn 2013 – Photo by Rosalie Leng

A Forest Summer's Day
Spring 2014

Now the blue-black beetle
Staggers its zigzag course
Shining in the morning sun,
And the dapper thrush seeks the source,
Head cocked, of its wriggling prey
In the dawning of a summer's day.

From the bracken, a sinuous adder
Winds its weaving way
To bask in the morning sun,
And the wary deer sniffs the air,
Ears alert, disturbed from where it lay,
In the warming of another day.

In the heather, clouds of buzzing bees
Follow their yo-yo dance,
Honey-sweet in the mid-summer sun,
Causing the purple heath to hum –
In a duet with a lark perchance –
In the noon-tide of a golden day.

And the black crowned Stone-chat
Flutter its up-down flight
To perch in the heat of the sun,
Chattering "Click Clack" from its gorsey height,
So near, now there then out of sight,
In the drowsy afternoon of day.

Now shadows darken, as the summer sun
Sinks in a smoke-blue haze
To complete its circular run,
And flames the clouds, and fires the sky,
Glimmering green to purple gloom,
Then nightjar darts to catch its prey,
In the owl-call twilight of a
Forest summer's day.

Wrinkly Ramblers Walk Tall
Autumn/Winter 2014

Wrinkly ramblers walk tall,
Retired and ready to have a ball.
You've bought your boots – what else to wear?
Would it be better to go just bare
As weather news is, some rain some shine?
No, others may think you're out of line!
And beware the bridges designed to pitch
Wobbly kneed walkers into the ditch!

Wrinkly ramblers walk tall,
But pride goes before a fall!
Novices at mounting stiles,
Find it's one of ramblers' trials.
There's "rockers", "leaners", and "Methuselahs",
Await to trip us on the top bars.
These lurk in fields surrounded by mud,
Too rapid descents, end … Splosh! Thud!

Wrinkly ramblers walk tall,
But now and then it's a very close call.
Many a walker loses his cool
Crossing a field with a very large bull.
He sees those fierce eyes and thinks he's the prize.
Then wrinkly rambler becomes a scrambler
And walks very small, invisible … <u>not</u> tall,
No pride in height when in panicky flight!

Wrinkly ramblers walk tall,
But if your cheeks begin to pall
Or are suffused with a purple hue,
Mobile owners will take the cue
To give the medics an anxious call.
Before you've time to reassure all …
Off on a stretcher your body they'll haul!
P.S. Do Wrinkly Ramblers walk tall When the pub is their last call?

The Vachery in Spring
Spring 2015

Verdure soft and dappled light
Await you in the Vachery,
A magic floral world
Of whispering trees and tranquillity.
Iris bloom amongst the reeds, around
The header pool, where gushes
Water in shining sheets, all pearled,
In sparkling falls it rushes
On, down the ferny ghyll.

Beside the path, from the Vachery heights,
The chuckling water flows
Playfully, tumbling into rocky pools,
Down the leafy gorge, into the hollow
Where brown lakes wait – sun-speckled. Still.

At the foot of the valley Primulas, bright,
Grow proud and erect from the watery soil.
Rhododendrons, gnarled and tall,
Lean o'er the lakes. Their blossoms fall
And float in roseate clouds, serene.
All nature is in harmony
In the valley of dappled light –
It's spring-time in the Vachery.

Magical Illusions
Autumn/Winter 2015

Magical illusions,
In the wandering wisps of the autumn mist,
Creeping gently down the valley sides,
Embracing heather, dark and crisp,
Tracing twigs and leaves in silver.
Now through the shifting swathes of mist,
Like curtains opened, shafts of light
Across the forest landscape slide
To where a mist cloaked valley hides -
Transforms it to a lake, mysterious, wide;
The forest ridge is now a mountain range,
A mirage …
Tricks of light, mystical and strange,
In the autumn mist.
Now the naked oak and birch reveal
Their skeletal beauty, as delicate as lace,
And robins sing, from their dewy twigs so fine,
Songs of whimsy and wistfulness to heal …
In the wandering wisps of the autumn mist,
Magical illusions.

The Four-Legged Forest Conservators!
Spring 2016

It's spring. Watch out, the animals are out!
From "Hollies" the Forest slope slides
Gently towards the Downs and on the rides,
Etched and sunlit, cattle shapes appear,
And everywhere –
Are sheep, blobs of cream, far and near.

Watch out, the sheep are out!
The forest road is all a-bustle
With woolly bolsters all a-hustle
On spindle shanks, tip-toeing here,
Then there, eager to browse the spears
And new shoots on the grassy verge.

Watch out, the cattle are out!
In the golden gorse, muzzles munching,
Mild bovines stand, leaves a-crunching,
Boot polished hides and long lashed eyes,
They calmly graze, show no surprise
When noisy dogs suddenly emerge.

It's Spring – Watch out, the VIP grazers are out,
Conserving the forest is what they're about.

Four-Legged Forest Conservators – Spring 2016 – Photo by Rosalie Leng

Ashdown "Forest", an enclosed area for hunting in Norman times, was given in 1372 by Edward III to his third son, John of Gaunt, Duke of Lancaster, and became known as "Lancaster Great Park." Commoners were permitted to graze their pigs and sheep in the clearances.

The area was mined for iron even before the Roman occupation. In the 16th & 17th centuries the Wealden iron industry was the centre of production nationally. The industry required the regular coppicing of woodland to produce charcoal for iron smelting which kept large areas clear of trees.

Treeless areas became lowland heathland but have decreased due to lack of grazing; it is now a rare habitat. It needs conservation because of the creatures which inhabit it; the Dartford Warbler, Nightjar, Woodlark and about 5000 species of invertebrates; butterflies, beetles, and bizarre species like "slave-making ants" and many species of Dragonfly. Some rare plants need conservation. Grazing animals do the job of keeping the "forest" open which allows heather and gorse, and the creatures that depend on this habitat, to thrive. 60% heathland/40% woodland is the best balance.

Hip, Hip for the Haw
Autumn 2016

Late September heat,	Boots off feet,
	Our picnics eat.
	Life is sweet!
Blackthorn low	We pick the sloe.
	Beware and know,
	Thorns also grow,
But worth the woe,	For Gin and Sloe
	We'll not forgo!
Hip and Haw,	Well I'm not sure
	If I should gnaw upon a Haw.
If I take a sip,	Upon my lip
	Of syrup of sweet Rose Hip,
	Recalls the War, so say no more.
But now the Haw.	Can we ignore
	The roseate glow of the Haw?
Should I abhor -	A cautious gnaw?
	Maybe it's not "hip"
	To be a Haw!
But I'll have a go,	At Liqueur of sloe!
	Slurp and sip, Shlurp, Shlip …
	Haw! Haw! Hip! Hip!
	Just another nip …?
And the **last**	Tiny sip!

A Walk from Camp Hill
Spring/Summer 2017

Pine crowned – Camp Hill's furrowed brow
Is softly greening now.
Its rutted tracks still with ragged sedge
And dingy heather edged.
But the mighty sun has pledged
That soon dark heather's bells will ring … and sing
To the sound of Summer
Of bees, humming … hummer.
Then honeyed breath
Of purple hazed heath
Will intoxicate the busy bees of Summer.
On Camp Hill's brow.

To Ellison's Pond

At hill foot – reed edged pond a-slough
Brownly gleaming now,
Its speckled depths entice, beguile
Passing dogs to swim awhile.
The paddled waters rippling surge,
Disturbs the life soon to emerge.
Then cows
Will stand hock deep,
Hock deep to steep
Their heated hides in mud thick pool … to cool
And alleviate the thirsty heat of Summer
In the pond a-slough.

Rest and Renewal
Autumn/Winter 2017

Autumn – When red apples rosily light
The orchard's rows, and purple sloes
Grow their misty bloom.
The dormouse is lining his winter room,
And squirrel admires his acorn haul
From old oaks whose leaves crisp, and fall.

It's Autumn – nearly time for all,
For all to rest –
To rest to live anew.

Winter – when day too swiftly slides to night,
Hugging the woods in its chill embrace,
Then badger strolls out in the shadowy gloom
To seek the worm in its earthy womb.
Still the darkening sky holds a fiery trace
When ghostly owl hoots its eerie call,
Then shivering mouse into shelter crawls.

It's Winter – and time for all,
For all to rest –
To rest and live anew.

A Prickly Matter for Pooh Bear
Spring 2018

We go with Pooh to stroll the forest tracks,
View the distant hills ablaze with golden gorse.
"Distance lends enchantment"
Thinks Pooh, a memory of remorse
Recalls a landing on his back
On golden gorse!

Within the golden gorse the spider builds its traps,
Scaffolds so strong only break with heavy force -
The Exmoor pony pushing,
Its neck leant against the gorse,
Ignores the painful prickles
To nip off the source.

From the golden gorse the Stonechat "snaps",
Perched, the Dartford Warbler sings its raspy song.
From the blooms exotic scent
Wafts, of coconut, fragrance strong.
Blooms for all seasons,
The golden gorse!

Gorse – Photo by Rosalie Leng

Friends' Clump
2018

Before the pines,
Foot-worn and ditch-surrounded,
A grassy space with views to satiate,
Of the blue and distant Downs.

Beneath the pines,
Shaded and needle-carpeted,
Somnolent sheep rest and ruminate,
Still aware of danger sounds.

Around the pines,
Picnicking families frolic and feast
And patient dogs drool and anticipate
The releasing of their bounds.

From the pines,
Walkers and joyous dogs descend
The valley and halfway, hesitate
To view the beauty that abounds
All about,
Friends' Clump.

Friends' Clump – Photo by Pat Arnold
Note – Information board in picture.

Under forty miles from Marble Arch lies Ashdown Forest in the High Weald Area of Outstanding Natural Beauty; it is designated as an Area of Special Scientific Interest. The largest area of open countryside in south-east England, it is managed by the Board of Conservators and run by the Forest Superintendent and her staff, plus volunteers, who maintain it for public enjoyment and scientific research. The Forest dates back to 1372 when John of Gaunt was given it as a hunting ground by his father, Edward III.

The Society of Friends of Ashdown Forest was founded in 1961 and planted 'Friends' Clump' of pines in 1973 to mark The Year of the Tree. Other clumps have been planted to commemorate many different 'occasions'. The Friends arrange 'bird' walks and some talks advertised in the Forest News.

For very many years Rosalie Leng has been a very keen supporter of the, in many ways important, Ashdown Forest. After 27 years as Information Volunteer at the Forest Centre her dedication was recognised when she was presented with this certificate of thanks by the Board of Conservators.

2 - ROSALIE'S OTHER POEMS

Rhymer in Residence

"Rhymer in residence"
I write lines of nonsense,
Embedded with ramblers who know
That I try to be lyrical
But am only comical,
And nothing Byronical
From my pen ever flows.

For me it is 'tragical'
My lines are not magical.
My thoughts may be spiritual,
But the rhymes are nonsensical –
Where did Clare and Keats go?

With fine words poets 'paint' ...
But my rhymes are just quaint!
Nature's beauty and rapture
I cannot capture
With my plebeian words –
It ends up absurd!
When will my words dance and glow?

Are my words appealing,
Is there homage and feeling?
Creating a picture
Of earth's great splendour?
No! With rhymes so trivial
The result is ... convivial,
Causing chuckles of "Ho, ho, ho."

I despair, I declare,
I will never get there.
My pen is perverse,
Writes only poor verse –
But in prose it takes flight
In words fulsome and bright
And imagination is all aglow.

But I still should aspire
Though my verse is quite dire,
If <u>some</u> are amused.
But I cannot compare or ever confuse
Rough rhymes with poetic muse.
The poems I read may one day inspire
A creative muse – and I'll grow.

May Blossoms

Delicate May, translucent light,
Pearly pink and froth of white,
Lime green leaves on beech and birch;
Bluebells cool on woodland floor –
A dappled carpet of bright azure –
Primrose pale, mauve violet, slight;
All these wonders are our delight
In fulsome May, blossomed bright.

ENTER - New Age EXIT - In Rage - 1994

There's this shiny black screen on my desk.
I throw a switch. What does it say?
"Welcome to Windows", <u>not</u> "Have a G'day"
Clickety-click – gives a message succinct
But I haven't a clue. Do give me a hint
How to open this File – just wait awhile.
Press that button there and what will appear?
Oh! Not again!

There's this black magic box on my desk.
I push the mouse – it becomes an arrow,
Some icons appear, but how do I know,
Clickety-click, which one I need,
I haven't a clue which will succeed
In giving me "Word". Oh! How absurd –
I've done it again!

There's this infernal machine on my desk.
I must master its magic today.
There's no time for rest until I make it obey.
Clickety-click. "Please Dear, answer the phone.
Me? No I'm busy. Leave me alone.
Time for tea – Can't you see –
It's been and gone and done it again!"

There's this Marquis de Saade on my desk.
It calls me all hours of the day,
So I've sent all my good friends away.
Clickety-click. I'm yours to Command.
Edit, Print, Move. What's your demand.
I'm your slave. Please Save me, Save.
I won't do it again.

There's this black nightmare thing on my desk,
And there's a Spreadsheet now on my bed.
I cannot sleep for the dreams in my head.
No **Escape**, no **Option**, must **Enter** again.
Clickety-click. Lines converge, commas dance,
Words wriggle, some advance.
Lost CONTROL. SHRINK, HELP.
Crash. And here I lie like a dead fly.
Wipe out - I wonder how, I wonder why.
RESTORE me again … to sleep.
Clickety-click. EXIT.

My 80th - February 2010

Eight plus 0, well don't you know
It's not time to be sage or behave my age –
It's get up and go and never say "no"
To a ripping lark, like a ride in the park
On a white llama in my pyjamas!
I can do what I like on a motorbike,
Wearing red leathers and a helmet with feathers!
I can go to the proms wearing long "combs" …
So I'll never say no to a spiffing suggestion
Though I may feel like dough and have indigestion,
As eight plus 0 will too soon be 90
And time to be sage and behave my age. Well maybe!

They Came for Tea - 2010

The visitors from hell,
They rang the bell
At four.
She gave them tea
In the conservatory,
Sandwiches and cake,
And now it's after six!
He gave them wine and cheesy bix,
Now it's all 'nostalgics'!
Oh woe! Oh woe!
How can they take
So long to go?
She gave them home-made soup and bread.
Oh dread! Oh dread!
It's nearly nine.
At last … they're going to the door.
Oh no! Oh no!
Their car won't go.
The visitors from hell
Are looking for a bed!
Put them down in Richard's shed
And firmly lock the door.
Those visitors from hell,
They came to tea
And stayed to dine.
Now they'll never be seen no more, no more!
Never be seen no more.

Mystic Masseur

She lay, her flaccid form
On couch, forlorn
Now, like a heap of dough
To be kneaded from head to toe.
Muscular, kind masseur, Oh!
Please don't pinch and pummel so.
This body is valuable – vintage, you know,
Four score years – and more to go
If you will leave some limbs intact.
Oh, golly gosh I heard a crack
But, yes, you really have a knack
For pushing joints completely back,
And stretching limbs as on a rack!
Now I feel taller ... You look smaller!

Thank you, thank you, kind masseur,
I'll make a date, ... in the far future.

Doves

Doves are lovely, Pigeons are portly,
And ne'er the twain shall meet!
Oh, fat grey pigeon whom nobody loves
Why do you think you are a dove?
Doves are elegant, white and pure,
You're the opposite, that's for sure.
You waddle and gobble and constantly woo,
Then you get in the bath and what do you do?
You drink and prink
In the water, then ... Poo!

Fun at Eighty-one!   2011

Now I'm eighty-one
I can be rude … but it's not much fun
If friends start to shun
Me. What else to be done?
On roller blades and dressed like a Nun,
Tear down the High Street?
Now that **could** be fun!

Now I'm eighty-one
I can wear purple. But it's not any fun
If my well matched mascara
Begins to run.
What else to be done?
On a red quad-bike zoom through the town?
Now that **would** be fun!

Now I'm eighty-one
I could be wise – but that's not fun.
I dislike the humdrum
So what haven't I done?
On my steed "Pegasus" ride to the sun?
But I'd burn like a bun.
Now that **wouldn't** be fun!

Now that I'm eighty-one
I can be (more) daft – but I know what **is** fun.
It's here with the family, … and the things **they've** done;
The warmth of love; the lives just begun;
Our presence together,
Now that **really** is fun.
(And I could always buy a ferret
To race and wear a flat cap!)

Sue at East Dean
My friend Sue and her dog

T'was brillig and our Bert and Sue
Did leap and frolic on the Green!
Such skittish 'larks' have ne'er been seen
By the Mome Raths of East Dean.
All mimsy are the things they do –
I swear that this is really true –
They gyre and gimble all the time
And their 'outgrabe' is quite sublime!

Clyde House School
My old school

There was a school of small renown
In an ancient seaside town.
It taught young ladies manners – not 'nowse'!
Could it possibly be Clyde House?

Clyde House 'gells' were so correct –
Well-mannered and quite circumspect.
And elocution was always taught
To all who said what they 'didn't ought'!

When Clyde House boys began to grow
And young ladies' curves began to show,
To save the 'gells' sweet innocence
Big boys must leave – t'was common sense!

Now Clyde House girls and boys unite
Annually, and they rarely fight!
Now wrinkled, crinkled with life's endeavours,
May Clyde House 'Crumblies' go on forever!

Winter Lingers Long - 2009/2010 March

Winter's sharp and icy bite
Still holds us in its greedy jaws
Unrelenting, full of spite,
Loath to let us go,
Jealous of the South West wind,
From its craw it spits more snow.

But like a mouse from hibernation,
Seeking signs of Spring,
I, keen to help creation,
Dart defiantly from my door,
Hearing song-birds on the wing,
Feel the urge to sow and grow.

A pot, full bellied, sparkles brightly,
With dainty snow-drops overspills.
The crocus, sun warmed, opens sprightly,
But daffodils dormant linger long.
There's a flurry of feathers, an urgency,
A cadence of glory, Spring sounds I know.

Soon, soon, I whisper, Spring is near.
Soon, soon, my birch, bare moonlight white,
Will hide, full-dressed in green to wear.
.The twisted branch of the willow tree
Will dance in its delicate finery,
And to the Southerly wind bow low.
Soon, soon … I know.

View Through the Window Early March 2011

I see … The first Spring prophets are a-shining,
Little white Nuns nodding demure,
In green gowns, petite and pure,
In the frost rimed grass sparkling.

Purple and gold crocuses are rejoicing,
Like rich-gowned kings, with crowns royal
Raised to the sun, from the dark soil,
For the transient rays their colours to glory.

Now golden trumpets shout a fanfare
"Spring is here". The willow joyfully sweeps
Its ribbons of green, which swing and leap
Above the grass, in the soft wind there.

I see … Violas, orange and mauve now smiling
Veined and painted with hair streaks beguiling,
So subtly adorned. But beware snail horned –
See leaves edge-fretted. Gardeners be warned!

Now, busy birds are posturing, beaks a-pecking,
But where is the warmth, enticing and beckoning?
Not yet, not yet, not in my reckoning!

To my cardis, woollies and scarves I cling
Till it's safely time for clouts to fling!
Repeating, repeating last year's Spring,
I dream of my days of gardening.

Spring 2012

Drip, drip, plop, plop.
When will it ever stop!
April, May, June, July.
It makes me cry, "oh why, oh why,
Should hose-pipe use be banned!"

The sky is grey, the wind is cool,
And I could drown in that big pool
Outside our front door step
And the postman vanished in its depth!

Drip, drip, plop, plop –
Here comes another crop
Of showers of bloody rain!
Can anyone stay sane?

Plop, plop, drip, drip,
I must take a firm grip
Of shovel, brush and pail.
Here comes a tide of snails!

Pitter patter, running water,
Soggy plants, all is slaughter
In our comely plots – disaster,
In our house, falling plaster!

Drip, drip, plop, plop.
When will it ever stop?
Summer's gone in tidal rain,
The rainbow's in the sky again.
August beckons through the mist.
Could that month be "sunkist"?

Raindrops are falling on my head.
Not a comfy thought, but dread
That Noah's Ark is leaving soon …
And – there may not be much room!!

An Ode to Odious Weather - Spring 2013

Why is this weather so infernal?
Why is this winter so eternal?
It seems there's not a single kernel
Of hope for a better "Climate Change".

Jan. and February were cold and 'doomy',
March is cold wet and gloomy,
But if the birds begin to sing,
I wonder what will April bring.

All last year was "plip, plop, plop"
Now this year, will it ever stop?
Last March was warm and 20C,
But this march is snow a-plenty,
Drifts "oop North" of fifteen feet,
In the South much rain and sleet,
Don't go West, the floods are dire,
River waters rising higher,
Hillsides awash, houses collapse!
Will Summer be drier? …
Perhaps, perhaps.

Beastly, Easterly, wild and wet,
Blizzards in the North, no Spring yet.
Snow whirling, driving. It's all set
For cars to be stuck, and a sure bet
That snow on the lines will make it get …
Much worse!!

Awash, Drowning not Waving! - Winter 2013/14

Again drip, drip, plop, plop
Again, when will it ever stop?
December, January and Feb,
Will the floods never ebb?

Hurricane winds, monstrous seas;
Cliffs collapse and blown down trees;
Farmland drowned in tidal rains;
Rail lines ripped and submerged lanes!

Storm force gales whip trees to frenzy,
On the coast, the turbulent sea
Hurls itself with dashing fury
Crashing, thrashing, lashing land.

But, inland, rivers wrought disaster,
Flooded homes with filthy water.
All is ruin, doom and dire
For those whose lives are in the mire.

But now the month of March is here!
The clouds above the sodden earth
Have gloriously given birth
To a long forgotten star,
And the earth is filled with sudden mirth
And wonder for that sun afar.

But has the drip, drip, plop, plop,
Really come to a stop?
Is Noah's Ark high and dry,
And can we answer the how and why?

The Holy Spider April 2015

I decorate my corner
With drapery so fine.
To remove all flying pestilence,
All things of insect kind,
I weave in silk so very dense
An intricate design.

My skill was never recognised,
But, Christmas Day last year
I lookéd up and saw a star,
(I knew this was a sign).
It was not shining from afar –
But in my web so fine!

Now in bonny April,
The star, it shineth still,
(This is my recompense).
To all it beareth witness,
I worketh hard all day
SO all who labour will be blessed –
Remember, those who dine! …
ONLY at TRITON this star will surely shine!

Explanation – A small, glittery **Christmas** *star caught in an undusted cobweb was noticed at a family* **Easter** *lunch!*

Winter 2015/2016

I feel like a mole in a hole –
Not a dormouse in cosy oblivion.
I sniff the fresh air,
Hopefully. It is wet and cold,
My hole is warm and I'm not bold.
Is the sun in oblivion too?

I feel like a mole in a hole –
Afraid to go out, I do not dare
Now the East wind has hold.
But life is happening, I'm told.
Is the sun in oblivion still?

I'm still a mole in a hole –
Not a dormouse in cosy oblivion.
I'm so bored I could swear
That my paws will decay
If I spend one more day –
I'll explode in my hole
And be an Ex-mole.
A mole with a hole for a soul!

A Springtime Walk

We talk and walk and walk and talk.
Breathe the breeze and look, and care,
Excited that …
Leaf buds are springing,
Blackbirds are singing,
Yellow brimstones are winging,
Hark! …
On the heath stand a'listening,
It's the song of the lark.

We walk the woods and smell the bark,
Hear the trees and stop and stare,
Look! …
Windflowers sparkle in dappled light
Bluebell buds are a mauve –blue glimmer,
The blackthorn, now a tracery of white,
And birch leaves gleam in a sun-bright shimmer.

We walk the ways and pause and gaze
On deer in woodland, unaware.
And see! …
The lordly beech crown hazed with green,
Humble violets on primrose banks –
Now, for these wondrous sights we've seen,
I give God thanks,
For the promise of life renewing,
For the hope that is ensuing,
For the joy of Nature sharing
Walking, talking, looking – caring!

The High and Mighty Bed – Dec 2009

For a long time I've said
"We do need a new bed.
This one has years twenty
With curves more than plenty,
But curves concave
Never will save
The health of my ageing back
In need to lie prone in a comfort zone.

So we've got a new bed
And I would really dread
To fall from its height on my head!
T'is as high as the sky
You need wings to fly
To roost in its memory foam.

So, resting in our mountain lair,
Relaxed, content … I became aware
Of a chemical pong,
Unpleasantly strong.
What could it be?
I had to see.
From sniffing here and sniffing there,
I thought I found from whence it came.
Fling wide the windows and the doors
Now I know what is the cause!
Now icy blast sweeps through my hair!
But odour's gone so what do I care.
New foam on mattress was to blame
If you thought other – that's your shame!
Now I lie up here in pure mountain air!

Our wondrous bed has drawers galore,
Two his, two hers, equals four.
Oh, what glee! What fun to see
How much stuff we make them store.
There's pants, vests and some sweaters,
No! Rugs and sheets would be far better.
Pillows and blankets have filled this space,
Now there's no more room to place,
All those things I'll use no more!

How can I rest in my eyrie
With a problem so very dreary,
Knowing that in the depths below
Where common sense has feared to go,
There are splendid drawers so full,
Atlas, himself could not pull
Them out, so I am about
From my pinnacle to leap out
To completely re-arrange,
Everything will have to change!

In the morn, with eyes so bleary,
With a bed so good,
Why am I still weary?

Have Some Madeira
A cautionary tale of a tout - July 2008

Let's go to Madeira, m'dear,
Climate change has reached Sussex, I fear,
The sun shines on that island, I hear,
So we'll head for the skies that are clear,
We're off to Madeira, m'dear.

We've arrived in Madeira, m'dear,
And, guess what, it's much hotter here.
When a tout stopped Ron, did he swear?
No, he physically showed, "You're too near!"
The Tout cried, "To push is so rude!"
Ron said, "Your manners are crude."
The tout calls, "Because you're so old and so sear,
I'll forgive you this time, do you hear!"
With a smile, I say, "This is Madeira, m'dear."

The Tale of the Madeira Tout

A persistent tout meets a resistant senior.

We walk on the prom on a beautiful day.
A tout bars our way
And we know what we'll say,
"Not interested, no thanks,
We know your pranks."
Tout persists,
We resist
I walk on by,
There's a loud cry,
"It's rude to push – and why?"
Ron retorts, "you're too bold
And see what I do when I try!"
Did Ron's hand, touch, push or shove?

It matters not a jot,
Touts deserve their lot,
But I heard the tout shout,
"I'll forgive you, because you're so old!"
There is now no doubt,
This gives us the clout
To push and to shove,
Swear and leap about,
Throw dignity in the gutter,
To snore loudly and splutter!
Not slow to anger or sage.
Oh, what joys there are in old age!

A Weary Walker's Wail

"Over the hill and far away"
Is the distance between me
And a cup of tea!
But it's puzzling me still
Why "Over the hill"
Is a term for old age.

How can it be?
It's a lie patently!
My legs and my brain are telling me –
It's up, up – never over and downwardly.

"Over the hill"?
Which hill? What hill?
Always climbing, striving
Till, we are still –
God's will
There will always be ... yet another hill.

Transient Spring

March – Whipping winds toss dead leaves high
And rip the clouds which mask the sky.

April – Breaths life into skeleton trees
And dresses them with budding leaves.

May – Sparkles the hedgerows in bridal white
And bees are busy in humming flight.

"Too soon" June –has the shortest night!

Then – longed-for Spring has passed us by,
Gone, in the blinking of God's eye.

The Happy Wanderers

We are the happy Wanderers,
We wander far and wide.
We get pleasure,
Beyond measure,
Walking the countryside.

We are the chatty Wanderers,
It cannot be denied,
No climb endeavour
Slows talk for ever –
Just makes the chat subside!!

We are the muddy Wanderers,
We wonder with each stride,
How much better
Than getting wetter,
To have stayed by the fireside.

We are the wrinkly Wanderers
In our efforts we have pride.
We have reason
To love each season,
As time does not abide.

High Weald Waddlers

High Weald walkers we be,
All sizes and ages are we,
As we walk a few miles
We remember with smiles –
There's a pub at the end with Harveys!

Greetings to High Weald Walkers

Whacky, Weird Walkers are We

Indomitable walkers we are
We hide under trees for a shower,
We say, "Oh, what fun",
Although looking glum,
Such indomitable walkers we are.

There was a walker from Tralalee
Who rambled through the green Vachery.
She fell in a pool
Said, "Oh, it's so cool!!"
That unfortunate walker from Tralalee.

There was a fit walker from Br'm
Who loved a strenuous run,
The marathon she's done,
Will she try a 'half-tun'?
That ambitious walker from Br'm.

There was a walker called Gnel,
From a bridge she slipped and fell
On her back – What a sight!
In a ditch – What a plight!
That uncomfortable walker called Gnel.

There are half-day walkers who choose
To go for a walk and a booze!
They sit in a pub
Talk, laugh and eat grub,
But their balance they never lose!

A Walker's Warning

When walking main roads, take care,
There are pavements you should be aware.
The curbs grow an inch or two,
Just when you thought you knew,
How high to lift your shoe!
Too late, you have rumbled,
Just as you stumbled
To fall on the pavement there!

Now give this warning its due,
Because we know of a walker, who
Whilst singing a song,
Fell completely headlong
On her face, which was black and blue.
The blood and the hue
Made her face such a sight,
She gave all a fright,
So they cried, "Begone, do,
See the hospital crew –
Next time take care who you fight!"

A Talker's Warning! **Hyperbole**

The Cherry and the Apple tree,
Both are fair and pretty to me.
Pretty fair, fairly pretty –
Words misused so frequently,
And *hugely enormous* are monstrously
Overused gratuitously.
        Today -   Double negatives are fine,
                        But you will always shine –
    With **Hyperbole!** *Absolutely.*
And you can be creative,
Changing noun to adjective.
It is done quite regularly
On Radio 4, but not Radio 3!
Fantastisational? *Absolutely.*
        Correct Grammar – What's that?
        Now isn't that *Old Hat?*
            Laying for lying, *Stood* for standing?
            Wrong tenses keep expanding! *Absolutely.*
And punctuate your word flow,
With "Y' know, Y' know, Y' know."
Freely use *organically,*
And, you know, *basically,*
You'll be cool. *Absolutely.*

Kushti's Last Summers 2002-2003
The year of our Golden Anniversary

You have all gone, my family,
Some hours have passed and I miss you so.
T'was a summer fantasy
Has left my memory aglow.

You broke my sad reverie,
But Kushti recovered to bestow
Her playful charm for all to see!
We cared so much – how could she go?

She stayed another year for me,
She knew I could not let her go
Before our Anniversary –
Then I had to let her go.

Time has passed, my tears still fall,
I loved you so but you have gone.
Still joyous adventures I recall,
Your zany personality,
So humorous, these memories
Stay always. To be forlorn
Would be to regret that you were born.

A dog so special still lives
Only a dog's life span,
But in that life gives
So much love – more than others can.
Kushti, your special life began
In '87, that memorable year
Of the Hurricane. It was clear
From your start to your end
In two thousand and three, that you were –
Special!! No other dog can transcend
Our wonderous dog, Kushti.

(She lived with us for sixteen and a half years)

3 – IRENE - ROSALIE'S MOTHER'S POEMS

Untitled

He came and stood behind my chair
I felt – I knew, that he was there.
All the air around grew colder
Was his hand upon my shoulder?
I heard the shrill peal of the phone
I turned and rose, I was alone!
When I picked up the receiver
My hand shook as though with fever.
They said that he had passed away,
Yet, I am sure he came today!

The Nightmare

A horror from the deep
Came over me in sleep,
With slavering of jaws
And tensing of great claws
It drew near!
Its torrid breath, a cloud,
Began my cheek to sear,
I cried aloud in fear!

A furry head was bowed
Above me, cat's soft paws
Invited me to play.
I woke to find it day!

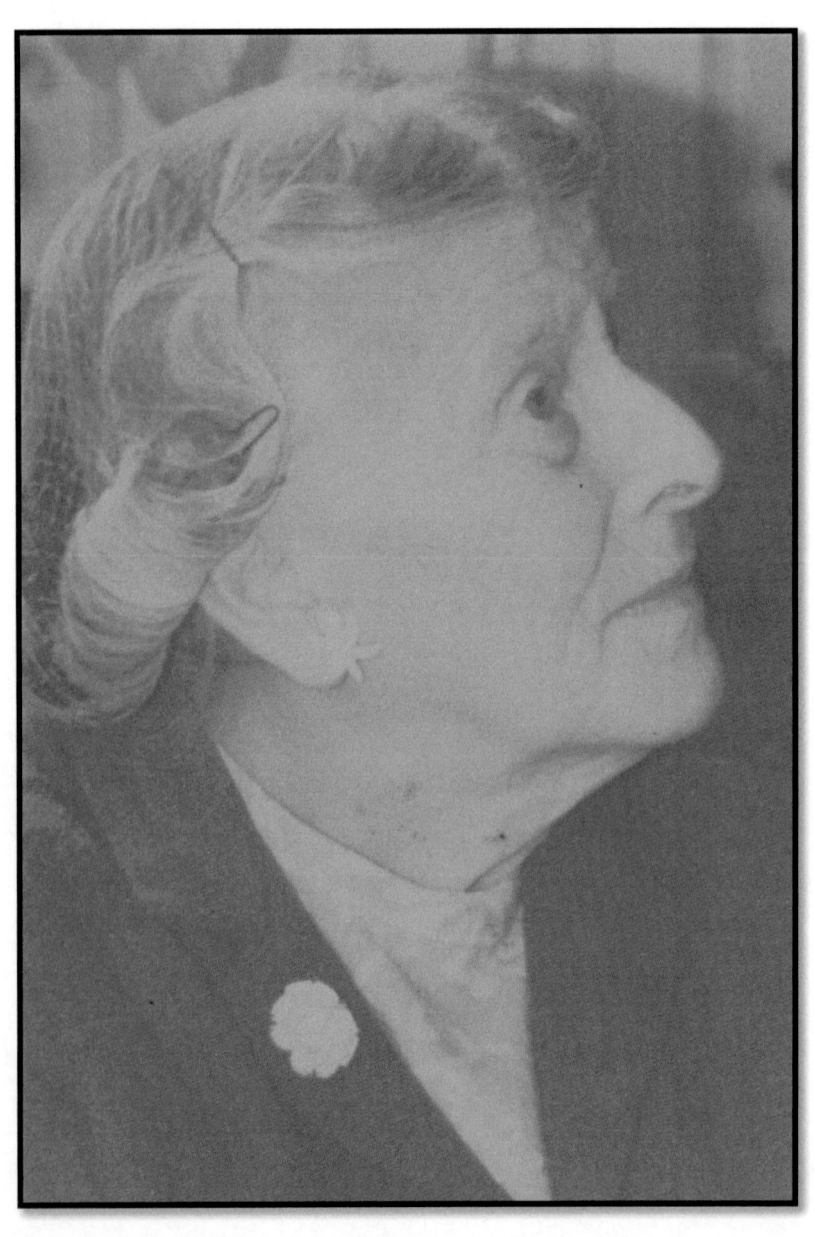

Irene Case (Née Davies) – Rosalie's Mother.

William Case – Rosalie's Father

Fear Hath Torment

Fear is a spear
To pierce – to sear.

Love is a balm
To heal, to calm

Fear is a rope
To strangle hope.

But
Love is but He
Who sets us free!

Fear's hands of ice
Grip like a vice.

Love will suffice
To melt the ice!

Gone

I could not stretch across the gulf
And touch your hair,
Nor could I half your burdens share,
I could not share your joys,
If joys there be
And so, I do not want to go
And climb the golden stair
Until you come with me.

To David - Rosalie's Brother

He is the spiders' friend
And in that friendship's cause,
With flies he'll often tend,
Those ever-ready jaws.

The Scourge

She seemed to be the scourge of God
And may have been a chosen rod,
Like prophet Jeremiah of old,
A sense of duty made her bold!
She "knew the truth", it should be told!
I suffered much - and so did she –
From this relentless honesty.
Now she has gone – I must forget
The judging eye, which haunts me yet
For when I see her once again,
We shall have done with grief and pain.
We two will meet with fond embrace
And I shall see her loving face.
Then we will read each other's eyes
Sweet questions will have sweet replies.
Dim visions will be crystal clear
And dried will be the bitter tear.

The Slug

She raised her happy horns to spy
The luscious cabbage, growing high …
Then spread her skirts to slide with ease
Towards the rows of David's peas.
He saw her come but let her be
"Because" he said "She's more to me
Than any cabbage bean or pea."

Abracadabra

Full-fleshed he danced upon the green
His pallid face wore a silken sheen.
I saw his patent leather toe
Snuff out the mushroom's milky glow.
When morning tore night's ghostly pall,
He vanished! Was not there at all.

Dreams

She seemed to come from out the wall
And walked towards me down the hall.
Her hands were clasped as though in prayer
And round about her frosted hair
She wore a grey cobwebby shawl.
She passed me by without a look
And went straight to the chimney nook.
I thought it was so very queer
That she should simply disappear.

Another Dream

I dreamt that I rode on a great winged steed
We galloped o'er clouds at a breakneck speed.
Stars and galaxies all rushed by
As we clove our way through the indigo sky.
We seemed to aim at the moon's white face.
How soon would we reach her at this mad pace?
Or shall I be riding for ever high
On snow-white clouds in this indigo sky?
And as I was giving up in despair,
I awoke and panted from my nightmare!

An Allegory

Once I saw a purple flower,
It was growing in my bower
And behind each purple petal
Sprang a tongue of golden metal
And with great velocity
It's tendrils wriggled up a tree,
Grasped a branch with ferocity!
I cried, "This thing must never be!"
I took my heavy strong pronged fork
And slashed its evil yellow stalk.
Then from its stalk and flower and bud
There spurted out black streams of blood.
I dropped my fork and ran away.
The horror haunts me to this day.

A Gardener's Lament

Towards the beds I long to hie
But **Not** the beds on which we lie.
Towards the pots my eyes will rove,
But **Not** the pots upon the stove.

My toil-worn hands have fingers green
Which ache to plant the runner bean
But conscience calls nor calls in vain.
I turn away from window pane.

I turn towards the unmade bed,
With drooping form and feet of lead.

The Baker – for David

Here's the baker man,
I can see his van!
He brings in his basket
Which seems like a casket
Of pastry-cook's treasure
For greedy folks pleasure!
Is that a bun?
Or a Sally Lunn?

As I feel choosy,
I'll have an Aunt Suzy,
She's one of the best
And has stood the test.
She's thought to be nice
By man and by mice.
Now shall I risk it
And have a choc biscuit?

Oh, I've got my eye
On that plump pork pie!
And last but not least –
Here's to the yeast
Which lifts up the head
Of our crisp loaf of bread!

A Wish

I wish that you were here to see
The bloom upon the Down's smooth cheek,
And in the sky that dusky streak
That lies across a rosy peak –
I wish that you were here with me.

To David

The daffodils sway and nod at the gate.
I step out quickly, I can scarcely wait
To see what has happened in one Spring night!
Have iris buds burst into light?
I know there'll be birdsong all around,
But will life be sprouting out of the ground?

Soon I must look for that friendly toad,
Under the bushes will be his abode.
Hungry for food after long winter fast,
He'll come out of hiding, I shall see him at last!

These dear signs of summer I welcome each year
And watch for sweet life from the ground to appear.

Cats

Cats lie on their backs
When they want to relax.
They fold their limp paws
With invisible claws
On a tummy of fluff
Like a powder puff.

If a mouse should pass
Those eyes of green glass
Would then open wide.
On all four paws glide
Till the mouse was inside
That tummy of fluff
Like a powder puff.

Dogs

There are no lies
In a dog's eyes.
When in disgrace
He'll sit and look
To read the book
Of Master's face.

If there's a trace of softness there
He'll cast off all his doggy care
And start to race
Instead of crawl.

Golden Retriever

He seems to be of noble birth
And treads upon the lovely earth.
He holds aloft, like knights of old,
A banner which is bright with gold.
He is of the elite
Two shining eyes so bright with love
And muzzle soft as velvet glove
And coat like ripened wheat.

Flowers

When all around is stygian gloom
With constant prophesies of doom,
What joy to see the roses bloom!

When milk of human kindness sours
And added years bring lessened powers,
I bless the innocence of flowers.

To My Valentine

Oh, youth is long a-dying,
And cupid's darts
Pierce ageing hearts
And sets them both a-sighing,
For bygone Springs
When feet had wings
And Beauty's flags were flying.

Yet kind looks from faded eyes,
Still can waken soft replies
And a gentle touch that clings
Can draw music from heart strings
For youth is long a-dying.

1956 – When her husband retired

This Spring's a happy one
Your freedom's almost won.
Set free from clerkly toil
You'll till the garden soil,
Or laze beneath the sun.

You'll wander on the rocks
Without your shoes and socks
And delve in pools, with joy
Just like an eager boy –
This Spring's a happy one –
Your freedom's almost won!

Convalescence 1973

Down the shining halls,
Round the rest room walls,
Echo the boasts of sore humanity –
For even pain may have its vanity!

Who suffered most
In that halting host?
How deep went the knife?
What danger to life?

Heads nodded or shaken –
Comparisons rife!
Down the shining halls
Round the Rest room walls
Echo the boasts of sore humanity.

To Bill – A Floral Border

The floral necklace round the grass
Lies there for all to see
But it is mostly meant for me.

And so I pause before I pass,
I pause and think of thee.
Were I with you or you with me
My love, how happy should we be!
Day after day it is sad cheer
To have you there, while I am here!

Ivan

There was a young boy called Ivan
Who said to his elderly Gran,
Without any ceremony –
"You are too soft with Jeremy,

You must give him a slap,
Don't take him on your lap,
He must be a tough man!"
"Oh, No, No!" said his Gran.

A Song to Ivan

He's a tough little chap!
A cute little chap!
And I do like the way
He wears his cap, cap, cap.

His nose **will** turn up,
His toes **won't** turn in –
And he's got such a
Cheeky little grin, grin, grin.

Rabbits

Their liquid eyes have no defence
Except the power of innocence.
Their ears can speak as well as eyes
When down they drop and up they rise!
A twitching nose completes their charm,
Oh, who would do a rabbit harm?

Sunset

Across the sunset sky
Clouds like pink fingers lie,
Below the clouds is seen
Some blue sky tinged with green.

But soon below the rim
The sun sinks, all grows dim.
Rocks, sand, sea disappear
And only I seem here!

Autumn

Upon the golden privet bough
The spiders' shroud like webs all clung
Like crystal beads the dew-drops hung,
It's sad to think it's Autumn now.

Grandad

Here's to dear Grandad
A boy on each knee.
A long time ago
There was only me!

Fiji (The poodle)

Enchanting "Pood"
Would it be rude
To ask you why
You spurn your food?

It's just my mood –
I must be wooed,
Or else I'll lie
Or stand and brood.

Memory

Oh, shut the door lest memory come in
To bring back to the mind forgotten sin –
And griefs which haunt dark corridors of Time
Where justice followed on the heels of crime.

Let me not see again the look that sears
Nor see anew dear faces wet with tears
And empty places goodness might have filled,
If I'd done the deeds I merely willed.

Let me forget the jibes of friends turned foes,
Who scorned me when I fell and never rose,
Until in mercy, strong hands from above
Reached down and lifted me to Light and Love.
Then I found peace of mind, unknown before.
Leave me this peace. Oh, shut the door.

Dalmation

He is a Dalmation
A kind of relation
To all sorts of hounds.
He will give leaps and bounds
After all things on wheels
Because he just feels
He is a Dalmation
And likes the sensation!

Kate and Meg
Meg is the family dog, a whippet

I am a Siamese
I do as I please
I don't mind Meg's jaws
I've pins in my paws!
If she holds me too tight
I claw and I bite.
Then she leaves me alone
And goes to her bone.

I am a Siamese
I do as I please!
While I "Miaow" good wishes
I dream of goldfishes
That swim in a bowl –
At the top there's a hole –
If I put in my paw
You will have to get more!
I'm a Siamese,
I do as I please.

A Poem

So strange and strong was her delight
It lent her face celestial light.
She felt transported to a sphere
Where God and Heaven seemed very near –
She knew that she was born again!
Joy was shot through with shafts of pain
And early pleasures seemed as dross
Beholding Him upon the Cross.

The Pine Wood

Oh, dark wood divine, with towering pine
Let me rest awhile in your shadowy smile.
Let me dream of my love!
With soft moss for bed and blue sky o'erhead,
While the sad, shaggy fawn with pipe all forlorn
Whispers low in my ear – lest the pine trees should hear –
Dreams of my love!

Tis here that we should, in this pine-scented wood,
In whispers reveal and with sweet kisses seal
Our mutual heart's love.
And the happy pine trees in the murmuring breeze
Would repeat it aloud to each hurrying cloud,
While to her on my breast, so closely pressed –
I would tell all my love! Tell all my love!

This is a much earlier poem which may have been written by Irene Case (neé Davis) or her sister, Ida.

The Ever Changing Sea

I

Thou ever-changing sea that rolls
And thunders on the drear
        Sea-Shore
Neptune's white horses dash along
And break upon the rocks with
        fearful roar
Oh! our ever changing sea —
Thou art a source of interest to me!

II

The sea-mew perched upon a lofty
Shrieks out a dismal discord
        rock
        to the waves,
That dash their spray up to the
        craggy ledge
Whereon she sits; calmly her feet
Far up above in the dark stormy sky
A group of shrieking sea-mews fly

Irene's sister, Ida's, poem, written in 1895 - The Ever Changing Sea

The Ever Changing Sea By Ida Davies in 1895 – This from her sister, Irene's hand-written copy of 1909.

Thou ever changing sea that rolls
And thunders on the drear sea-shore,
Neptune's white horses dash along
And break upon the rocks with fearful roar
Oh! Ever, ever changing sea –
Thou art a source of interest to me.

The sea-mew perched upon a lofty rock
Shrieks out a dismal discord to the waves,
That dash their spray up to the craggy ledge
Whereon she sits: calmly her feet she
Far up above in the dark stormy sky
A group of shrieking sea-mews fly.

And yet sometimes, oh, sea thy stormy breast
In summertime is lulled into repose
The sun shines down from the blue vault of Heaven,
From the calm sea a soft, cool sea breeze blows –
T'is then I love thee, lovely sea
For thou glad thoughts bring back to me.

The ripples flow upon the shore
The mist upon the sea laps low,
The vessels slowly move along
Amid the sunset's mellow glow.
Oh! Gentle ripples softly flow
O'er stones and gravel calm and slow.

How oft I stood and watched with raptured eye
The flock of snowy sea-gulls flying past
Or settling in the water, they float by.
Rejoicing in the splendour of the heavens
I stood and watched, till in the distant west
The sun had sunk, the sea-gull sought its nest.

The Sun

I

Through the long Winter with it's ice
Sat Phœbus shivering in his chariot, and snow.
All day with thick warm clouds his glow
He hid, till the approaching watery bright
Then to Olympus wrapped in mists he
To feast with all the gods the whole night

II

But now young Spring sits on old Winter's through
The snowdrops raise their heads, her steps throne
And glow returns the Summer's heat again,
And from the Heaven descends the cooling rain
And Phœbus rises with his golden car –
And challenges the lingering frosts to war.

At morn, the dim houses lie
Layers of golden mists built cumuli,
Like mountains 'gainst the brightening sky they stand
And seem the barriers of a distant land
Soon Phœbus rises from the red east
And spreads his rays o'er many 8 miles
verdant miles.

(copy of Ida's poem of February 1897)

Irene's sister, Ida's poem of February 1897 – The Sun

<u>The Sun</u> Ida Davies' poem written in 1897 – hand copied by her sister, Irene, in 1909

Through the long winter with its ice and snow
Sat Phoebus shivering in his chariot's glow
All day with thick, warm clouds his glory bright
He hid, till the approaching water of night,
Then to Olympus wrapped in mists he flew
To feast with all the gods the whole night through.

But now young Spring sits on old Winter's throne,
The snowdrops raise their heads her steps to greet
And slow returns the Summer's heat again,
And from the Heaven descends the cooling rain
And Phoebus rises with his golden car –
And challenges the lingering frosts to war.

At morn along the dim horizon lie
Layers of golden mist, built cumuli,
Like mountains gainst the brightening sky they stand
And seem the barriers of a distant land,
Soon Phoebus rises, from the red east smiles
And spreads his rays o'er many verdant miles.

Rosalie and Ronnie's Five Grandsons
Oliver, Kushti (dog), Alex, Frey, Crispin, Marvin

4 - ROSALIE'S GRANDSONS' POEMS

BY CRISPIN

<u>Dear Nana – Happy Birthday – 73 (2003)</u>

That sparkling smile from all those happy days
From walking the forest to sitting on those sunny bays
It's dark and wet at the Woodies camp
But still you smile like a radiant lamp.
It's now your birthday, you've reached 73 in age
The story of your life turns over a page.
So life will go on as it normally would.
One question I ask is if you could
Keep warming me with your sunlight charms
One day I'll be with you surrounded by palms.
(And he was in Trinidad in 2005)

<u>April '01 Aged 12</u>

Doody gallops through the heather
In the sunny Sussex weather
Looking out for a rabbit
Getting ready to grab it!
Now she's at home
Waiting for her daily comb,
A paw-paw here, a paw-paw there,
A massive paw-paw everywhere.
Stamp, stamp, waiting for food
Next to Nana she is stood,
She's getting forever slimmer,
But still waits impatiently for her dinner.

Twenty Meters of Land

For twenty meters of land
We lose our hands,
Amongst the battle heat
We lose our feet,
To honour our Queen
We have to be mean.
To die
We have to lie.
I thought, as I went over the top,
This war has got to stop.
I thought, I'd be remembered for ever more
If I came alive out of this war.
This was my downfall, was shot to the floor
Onto the barbed wire
I wish I wasn't a liar.

Crispin's poem 2001 - Aged 12

The silent night
The moon shines bright
Upon the motionless, tideless lake.
You see the ripples taking shape
Like thousands of slithering snakes.
Mountainous hillside silhouettes,
Far away sounds of noisy pets,
Crackling crickets struggle in a spider's cast,
The spider's gaining on them fast.
The sun peeps out over the hill
Casting light upon the turning wooden mill.

(Written on a family holiday in the Italian Lakes)

The Biggest Lie

The biggest lie
The soldiers die
To find our friends' fate
We have to wait.
The deafening guns
No one dares to run,
We're also not allowed to have fun.
The world's nightmare
OUR leaders don't care.
We need heroes
Not zeros
They tell us.
We answer,
"Oh don't make a fuss."
Being bad we're only lads,
Too much to drink
My friends think
That's how I got here.
Now it's my biggest fear,
The biggest lie,
The soldiers die,
The devil evilly laughs, but why?
Because the Sergeants are so sly
And do not hear the soldiers' cries.

Nana's House

On the way in the car,
The boys keep asking how far?
They can't wait to get to Nana's house,
To talk and wrestle on the couch.

Nana calls them as they come,
Listening for the dreaded sound of her grandsons' rumbling Tums,
She didn't come cycling this year,
The bumps were too much of a fear!

Taking "Doody" on the forest was truly fun,
We didn't care about getting cooked by the red-hot sun!

Playing football in the newly cut grass,
Crispin makes a perfect pass,
Marvin says that was great,
Now let's go and have a chocolate milkshake!

The final day has come too fast,
No hungry gannets for Nana to feed at last!
The boys say "Thank you Nana, thank you granddad",
And trail off feeling sad,
In the car music starts playing,
Over the top the boys are saying,
See you next time we are staying.

To Our Darling Nana - 2017
With love from Crispin and Gintare

To our darling Nana
Holder of super power!
Eternally young is she.

From White-Water rafting
To knit-wear crafting
There's no one so wonderfully free.

We love your diligent manners
And humungous glamour
You're a ray of sunshine in our hearts.

Your smiles and laughter
You're a "White lady" dancer
Our incredible, adventurous Grandma!

For Gintare – 2018

Butterfly Wings in my mind
Sending Shivers down my spine
To the stars within your eyes
And the infinity behind,

I'm Surrendering.

The Land of Shadows - Crispin Case-Leng

The great eye
Couldn't be a better spy
Our siege of Mordor
Wasn't a score
My life was spent,
I'll tell you how it went -
All his minions,
There was more than a million,
For every ten I killed
They killed twice as many men,
I'm only an elf,
An elf by itself.
The enemy were nearly all gone
We thought it was won
But then Sauron came with his magic staff
And he then began to laugh.
This was it; I strung my bow,
I really thought I was going to kill the foe,
But he swung that thing
And boy did it sting!
I would lie there for ever more,
Lie dead on the dusty floor
In the land of shadow -
The land of Mordor.

Leeds United's Title Dream - Crispin

Welcome to match of the day live,
To see if Leeds United can revive,
From their Champions League defeat,
Their football has become very neat,
So here we are at the last game of the season,
To see if Leeds can ease their treason,
It's Leeds v Man.U about to begin,
Leeds are hoping for a massive win,
The winner will take the premiership title,
So this game is very vital,
Man United down the wing,
They all have their minds on only one thing,
The ball's drifted in for the head,
The defence is surely left for dead.
It's one-nil, Man United celebrate,
The away supporters are thinking it's great.
It's the 84th minute,
Harry Kewell spins it,
It's in the top corner,
What a scorcher!
Great strike by Harry Kewell,
He really is a football jewel,
The last throw of the dice,
The fans are as quiet as mice
The free kick is taken, and is mistaken,
The title is there to be taken,
The final whistle blows,
Leeds forget their vows,
They've won the title,
This game was vital!

BY MARVIN

Midnight Breeze - 2001

It is a gentle whisper of a midnight anew,
A silent assassin at work.
It cannot be seen, but heard.
It is the chilling in your ear,
The 'whoosh' in the bush.
It is the moving of the still
Sometimes it makes us feel a chill
As we shiver in the night.
It can be a raging hurricane
Or a gentle push or pull.
Sometimes it makes some beautiful things
Or a disaster about to happen.
It is all these things – it is the Great wind.

(Written on family holiday in the Italian Lakes)

A Tribute to Amy – 2017

Amy, Amy, my sweetheart oh so true.
How I love my time with you
Your smile is such a treat for me
It says, will you be the man for me
And based upon that loving request
I'll freely say, you are the best.
You elevate my very soul, and bring me joy so untold
I cannot conceive of a future without you in it
That notion bleeds my heart, the many stitches needed so large
Before you, I thought myself so cool
But now the cloud of denial has lifted,
I realise before I met you I was not so gifted
To love and commit in ways I could not conceive
A man stumbling through life ignorant of his needs.
My life with you will never be a chore
Cos I'll always want to be your man, your rock, the one you adore.

BY ALEX

A Sea of Blood

We sharpen our weapons
We polish our shields,
We eat fresh boar
To the very nice core,
We go to say our goodbyes
To the ones we care for inside,
We train with swords and spears
For the overcoming terrible fears,
We pray in the morning, we pray in the day
We are going to war far, far away.
We pack our things
We leave our barracks
For we march away
This terrible day,
In the night
We train for the fight,
Men were groaning
While I was moaning,
Men would lie in their sand bed
Thinking of the battle some way ahead.

We throw our spears
As we run
We shout and charge
Everyone begins to barge,
Arrows and spears whiz through the sky
I begin to wonder if I will die,
Then I see an arrow rush past me
I turn to look at Fred
But he was lying there dead!
We won the battle
We are all glad
Apart from the men who died
Whose families are beginning to cry

The men who died in the war
Won't be fighting any more.
I take a steady pace through the tomb
I see my dead body just through the gloom
The blood is getting to me fast
But I'm nearly home at last.

We are free
We celebrate
I open my house door
My wife is crying on the floor
But she smiles at me once more,
I have some wine
Then invite some friends to dine.
We won the war
But I won't ever fight once more.

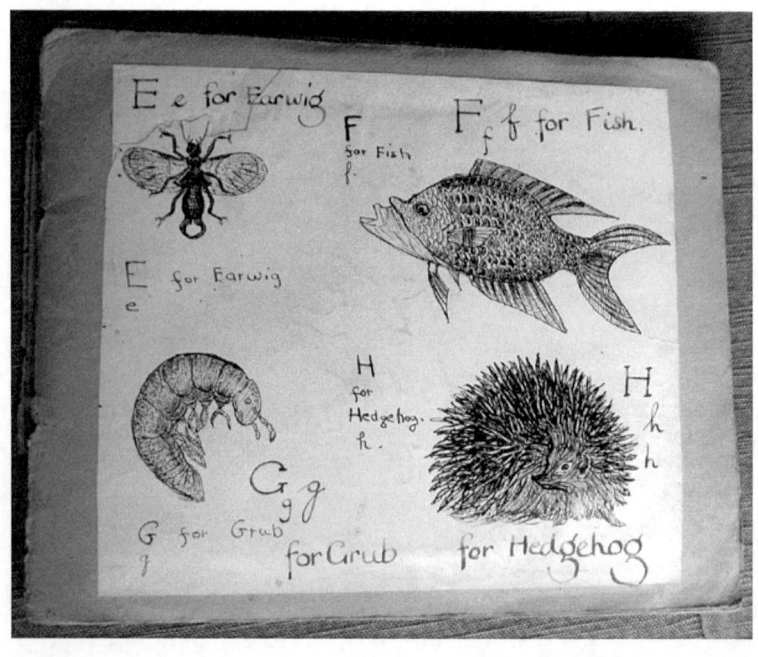

The Alphabet Drawn for her children by Irene, Rosalie's Mother

5 - TRIBUTES TO OTHERS FROM ROSALIE

Binoculars

By the river, by the sea,
On the heath and in the woods,
Frey would carry constantly,
Binoculars,
Slung from his little frame –
And it was not a game!

By the castle, by the lake,
In the marshes, on the hill,
It was compulsory to take,
Binoculars,
Slung from his little frame,
And birds were all the game.

On the cliff top, on the sand,
In the fields and through the trees,
Frey would always have to hand,
Binoculars,
Slung from his little frame.
Still birds were all the game.

Frey grew up and birds were spurned,
Then one flew in with plumage rare!
No feathers she, but features fair,
Graceful flight and long, dark hair.
Binoculars? How absurd,
Now she is in his frame!
This is a new, exciting game,
And life will never be the same!!

A Birthday Limerick
90 Mile Pilgrimage I also walked in 1996

There was dear lady, Pam Holt,
Whose memory became much at fault.
She started to walk a ninety-mile route,
But discovered her foot needed a boot!
That forgetful, dear lady, Pam Holt.
There was a walker of Uckfield
Whose feet became somewhat peeled.
Said Pam to her patient, "Oh, that can be healed,
With unction for sealing – we guarantee no feeling!
That caring, dear lady, Pam Holt.

Pam, your stamina and resolve are well known,
But some of us have less back-bone!
As next oldest, but new recruit,
The end of each route I longed to curtail,
But how could I fail – with you on my tail?
That indomitable lady, Pam Holt.

Pam, on one day of our pilgrimage
Became more energetic than sage –
She cried, "Jim, let's get hip," and started to skip,
"Together we'll dance, and forever we'll prance!"
That rash, jolly lady Pam Holt.

On the very last eve of our journey,
Some felt it was time for some jollity,
But it felt like bed-time, when Jim read us a rhyme,
And some crept into bed, But – Pam got up instead,
And joined in a wild game of hockey!!
That youthful, dear lady, Pam Holt.

There is a dear lady, Pam Holt,
May you never come to a halt.
We'll celebrate your birthday date,
Your qualities we'll like to emulate,
Excepting amnesia! Hurray for dear Pam Holt.

Tribute to Pat James - 1986 – 1996

Pat James, you started Mullberry,
And have put on many shows.
You have raised so much for charity
And shown so many clothes.
These photos of good clarity
Show how fashion comes and goes.

The audience feel expectancy
In spite of familiarity.
There's an atmosphere of gaiety,
As models of age disparity –
Also in style there's variety –
Parade with dash, or dignity.

Some pace with grace and fluency,
Some stride with taut ferocity,
Some whisk by with velocity!
Some with ease and informality.
Each to her own personality.

Girls unsure of their ability
Twirl with instability,
And question their own sanity
To do all this for vanity!

Some stiffly plod, some spin on toes,
All dressed in fashions which you chose.
We try to elegantly pose,
And hope for audience applause –
To prove they aren't comatose! And SMILE, SMILE!

Behind the screens there's hilarity,
As dressers fix belts and bows.
Thanks to your kind generosity,
Wine and encouragement flows! We SMILE.

Owing to this availability,
Cheeks glow and confidence grows.
Your staff show great perspicacity,
Handling the models like "pros".
And with tact and sagacity,
Advise when to powder one's nose.
And price labels remove with alacrity.
Are mistakes made, do you suppose. They SMILE.

So take a bow, hide your modesty,
Take the credit, as everyone knows,
For ten years in this locality
Of charity-raising shows,
Gaining esteem and popularity –
So well-deserved. Heaven knows!   We all SMILE.

With some more "word agility",
Maybe I'll come to a close –
So forgive the peculiar poetry,
Why didn't I say it in prose!!   You SMILE?

To Poppy

I'm a very important Dog,
I've appointments to keep all day
With garden Ghoulies who would assay
Our house, but I chase them away.

A brave and important Dog
Should be rewarded each day
With chicken, ham and some cheese, say.
But my clear requests they do not obey.
I'm a sad, disappointed dog.
In my very small basket I lay
And could not believe what I heard …
They said I'd get fat – that's absurd!

For Stephanie - March 2001

By the summer-time, dear friend,
May all your problems be at end.
The sun will banish rain
As God's blessing heals pain,
Your life will start again
And Sping's hope with ripe Summer blend.
I pray for this good time, dear friend.

Two poems for my neighbour's daughters.

To Tamsin and Lindsay - Easter 1996

If frogs liked dogs and dogs liked frogs,
Then fish could wish not to be on a dish,
Or a hen use a pen? Well, who knows when!
A bird sing a word? Well, how absurd!
That breaks nature's law, but I'm equally sure
That our "Funny Girls" who give us their whirls
Will always amuse; but we have to excuse
The squeals and the noise –
No better than boys!

Tis easy to bear as we care for their flair,
Their youth and their charm for "Crumblies" is balm.
We love and enjoy –
They love to annoy!
A hilarious pair, imagination they share,
So my hope as the years gain, that they'll never disdain
To come to our door
Or find "CRUMBLIES" a bore.

IF

If frogs like dogs
And dogs liked frogs
And girls had common-sense,
In this happy world of fantasy
Boys would be less dense!

If Mums were calm
Did not alarm,
Dads would stay quite sane.
In this happy world of fantasy
Grandmas could fly a plane!

Midori - You Came, We Saw, You Conquered! 2011

You came with smiles that filled us with delight,
You came with joyous love and hair shining bright,
You crossed the world from very different lands,
All for the sake of Frey, whose loving hands
And heart awaited to hold his lovely Midori,
Soon ... in matrimony.

Vivacious and gracious, with the beauty of a flower,
Capturing our hearts with the excitement of each hour.
It is clear that you are clever too – but, to join this family?!
The adjectives which spring to mind, are .. brave insanity!!
Love and welcome, Midori.

Marvin 2011

From beating up old Teddy Bears,
You've grown into a man who cares.
From lazy charm and youthful ways,
You've strived, achieved, deserve much praise.

May you always ride the wave,
And get fulfilment in the career you crave –
And, "with a little bit of luck" the N.H.S.,
Will supply your socks, I hope and guess!
_{Marvin "borrowed" family socks!}
But "Watch out, watch out,
There's a "Snailfinger" about ...!
In print.

I am so glad your written works did not end with "Snailfinger"!

Crispin for his 9th Birthday

Crispin is his name
Football is his game,
He has ball control
He can always kick a goal.
When they shouted "shoot"
He put it in with his boot.

Crispin is his name
Football is his game.
A modest boy he may seem
But he's the winner of his team.
When they shouted "score"
He put it in three times more.

Have fun at your football party – Lots of love from Nana.

Una Wareham's 61st

I've just heard, from a little bird
That you are sixty-one.
Why, that's absurd!
It's just occurred, though memory's blurred
I knew you at forty-one.

Then, I recall, you were still very small
With Child – your very first one!
Absurd.

Now you are still dancing
 I am still prancing, Absurd! Greetings from everyone

To David, the Loving Gardener

You are my dearest, only brother,
And now you've passed your 70th year,
I would like to say, "You're very dear,"
And that we grow closer to each other.

You are gentle, kind and tolerant.
You like to dig and sow the seed,
It matters not,
That your comely plot
Attracts the snail and slug to feed.
You like to nurture both pest and plant,
And feel it's cruel to cut a weed.
Most of your toil,
Upon the soil
Just satisfies the insects' greed.

You're happiest to hear the call
To help improve the garden's charm.
You dig up sods,
Remove the clods,
Heave up the slabs, not heeding body's harm,
You like to find black beetles, small,
Which in your care have no alarm,
For you, such bliss,
Although remiss,
To protect with loving balm.

You are fortunately blessed
With an artist's hand and eye.
You painted some views
In such lovely hues,
So good that Sue Watts had to buy.
Several more made that request,
Because of the colours in your sky.
So now's the place - To wish David Case
More birthdays with delicious pie
In the years which may pass by!

You loved "all creatures, great and small
For the Lord God made them all."

So Wise!

"Think about the birds flying in the sky"
You said, whenever mother scolded!
How did you know
That wrath is turned aside with soft replies?
You were so young, JJ, how so wise?

T'was all about a baby bird who hadn't learned to fly.
Frustrated when big brothers left the nest,
Growing up was slow
Eventually you had the confidence to try,
And you have overcome, JJ, you fly.

"Think about the birds flying in the sky"
I say, when I look out the window,
How would you know
My thoughts are turned to you with loving pride
At what you have achieved – you fly,
JJ, my son. You fly.

Our Visit to Family in California
A little ode to your daring Dad, after the style of Edward Lear

There was an old man of some age,
Who wished to be skittish, not sage.
He put on some skates
And went off at a rate,
That dashing old man of some age.

There was an old man, without aid,
Started to "roller-blade".
He tore up and down,
Which caused some to frown,
He just said, "I'm a jolly young blade."

There was an old man had a spouse,
Whose bum on a bike did arouse.
He said, "It's a cinch,
Her bottom I'll pinch,"
That naughty old man, we should dowse!

There was an old man, far too rude,
For harassment he could be sued.
He got in a tangle,
Legs and wheels at an angle.
"Taught a lesson," his wife merely cooed.

There was a young man and his son, *(Ivan & Oliver)*
Who saw this double-act done.
It caused them to laugh.
"It's better by half
Than Laurel and Hardy, my son."

There was a young boy and his Dad,
Asked Nana, "Was Grandad bad?"
She said, "Yes he was,
He fell down because …
T'will teach him a lesson, my lad."

You Gotta Have a Dream - April 2015
For Nick and Kali

Nick and Kali had a dream,
A scheme –
And finally a plan.
The internet led them to seek
And drive o'er dales and then the peaks.
Eventually they found their love,
A white 'ungeeky' camper van –
With a place to sleep
And a place to eat.
It even had a very nice beep!
It had shelves above
And shelves below,
And maybe a space for Granny to go,
And a little niche for Eddie the dog?
And more important –
It does have a 'bog'!

The Sad Tale of Maisie's Lost Tail
She had her tail shortened!

Ivan and Debbie fell in love,
A love that was deep and true.
And it was a very stylish marriage,
They could well afford a carriage,
But they were both 'half crazy'
As what did they go and do?

"Maisie, Maisie", why did we fall for you?
We're half crazy over the things you do!
You had a very stylish carriage,
But now your tail is damaged!
But you still look sweet,
Upon the seat of an armchair made for two.

(Maisie is a dog – a Vizsla)

Action Stations 2017

Oh, where have you gone,
My Nick and Kali?
You've gone to see dawn
In the West Country,
Spreading its golden gleam –
See dawn from your campervan,
Whilst having a cup of tea!

You've gone where the sky
Meets the turbulent sea,
Where, like the boisterous wind
You are free –
To live your campervan dream.
And is there a cup of tea?

And where will you go
Now you've sown the seeds,
To be free as the wind blows?
You'll go wherever that wind leads,
And still have your cup of tea.

To Eileen - With much love – Rosalie Jan 1996

What sunny days we had, dear Eileen.
In glorious gardens walked in shared delight
And saw the acer with its roseate leaves a-gleaming.
You stood by lily-padded lake, a-dreaming,
Showed no despair of your inner fight,
No self-pity to cause a blight.
How privileged I am, dear Eileen.

What golden days you had, dear Eileen.
On green fair-ways played, and shared success
With your beloved; acclaimed captain of the ladies team
You deserved to be - fulfilled a happy dream.
You showed only zest, always coped with stress.
No fair words can ever express
How privileged we are, dear Eileen.

What memories we have, dear Eileen.
Oh, memories mixed with joy and humour,
Recalling so many, more and more.
Joy, humour and courage, with love your core,
You enriched our lives – no friend was poor –
And your family, your love of life will store.
What memories we have, dear Eileen.

Now you have gone, our dear Eileen.
Your wish – no regrets for what might have been.
You made your peace and fulfilled your life,
Your duties done well, now no more strife.
Your life, but a drop, a ripple creates,
A ripple spreads out, never terminates.
So you have not gone, our dear Eileen.
In the hearts of your family,
In the hearts of your friends,
Your example is held, dear Eileen

Irene and John go West

You've left your cottage with a view,
You've left the hills of Sussex too,
You've left a hole – a "Hays' space" –
Was filled with friendship, warm and true,
For those you've left, they're quite a few.
You've left …
For family love, the bond which drew
Our kind friends to make their base
Now, in Wales, where 'tis your due
To enjoy life at a slower pace.

Irene will knit and sew, her wonders to fulfil,
John will create shelves, paint doors and cills.
Will they walk hand in hand up many hills?!
No! Those Welsh heights are sure to kill!
So slow as you go –
Watch the children grow,
In the family fun you'll have a share.
As you've always cared for others,
Let others return your care.

Eccentricity
Remembering Felicity

You can swim with the ducklings in the park,
Run naked through the daffodils, what a lark!
Go to Hurlingham Club for gracious tea,
Dressed all in leather outrageously.

You can visit a manor of the National Trust
And draw a moustache on a noble bust.
In your allotment grow nothing but thistle
Because you love the goldfinch's whistle.

You can ride your bike in and out of the Tate
And throw eggs at all the paintings you hate.
When all are in tears at the opera Tosca
You can jump up and belt out an aria.

Your partner in Bridge is annoyed with the score
You can just snore and annoy her much more.
And if you have the misfortune to swoon
You can dress in an inflatable balloon.

Everyone knows it's your eccentricity.
But beware! Take care to retain your memory.
Keep losing yourself, your 'cool' and your key,
And forget your home and its vicinity,
Then it might in reality be age and … senility..

A Tribute to Pamela who died 5.2.96

Pamela, you were my dear, long-loved friend,
Honest and true. There was never need to pretend.
In life's ebb and flow, we shared some joys, some fears,
Our rock of friendship based on more than fifty years.

Seeking recollection of happy memories
In dusty albums, my sorrow to appease,
Your face in youth smiled from a page, reviving the past;
But you are gone so suddenly, your earthly shackles cast.

In the chambers of my mind, I can visualise
Forty years ago, your face, serene, with golden eyes
Shining with mischief and irony, humour and quizzical,
To me the essence of your character in a mind-sight so physical.

Your own endeavours and success you valued naught,
Dismissed yourself as little worth, and ever sought
To praise others. But family and friends will ever value
Your real worth. You were clever, gentle, honest and true.

Pamela, oh Pamela, we have to comprehend
That your gentle personality does not really end.
Your eyes, your smile, your kindly acts, a permanence ensure.
Your modesty, wit, compassion, in memories will endure.

A Letter to Wendy from Rosalie - December 2012

You were a very special friend,
In whose company I liked to spend
Happy hours in which we talked,
Not of cabbages and kings,
But of bluebells on a walk;
The forest; gardens; varied things
And concerts – when the soprano sings
Would her voice sore up on wings?

How are you so lovable?
Is it your
Patience was so enviable …
Forbearance was so remarkable …
Gestures so individual …
Dress 'combos' so unusual …
Like red socks with skirt – enjoyable?

These are the ways

Dear Wendy

All loved your very special smile,
With genuine warmth, you could beguile
A gloomy mood to lift awhile,
And the world became a brighter place
When the light of your smile shone from your face.
But you are not gone.

And even,
The humble daisy was in your care.
The slashing mower was made to spare
Those starry heads

And shape them into a fairy ring!
And now on a sunshine summer day,
When daisies gleam like the Milky Way,
These thoughts of you will bring a smile,
And then, in the echoes of our minds,
We may hear you saying, gently, "There".
But now its meaning is … "I'm here,
I am only gone for a while."

To Wendy on her 70th Birthday – May 2009

Dear Wendy, you're a special friend,
Always willing your hands to lend,
To haul around our water hose
Sprinkle rows and rows of pots.
But now you're Seventy – who knows?
Fed up, you'll tie it up in knots!
A secret thought do you suppose?

We know at 70 life does not begin,
But face the world with a happy grin,
Wearing red socks and a purple hat
And a mini-skirt. What's wrong with that?
You can mow a circle round a daisy,
Now you're 70, it's not crazy.
So give a cop a wicked wink,
Because you don't care what they think!

Now you are sure and seventy,
Not silly, shy and twenty,
For a special lady,
Still time to live a-plenty.

Agile & Mobile with Style - Sept 2010 for Alan

When Spring's warm breath our skins delight,
Our hearts are full, our steps are light.
Then who, like March hares, leap each stile
And who of us lands in a pile?

When sunshine days bring violets mauve
And primroses in shady grove,
Who are they who pause awhile
To stare? No! – to use mobile!   Alan

When clouds roll dark and torrents pour
Upon our heads – we can ignore;
And who are they still wear a smile?
But – <u>who</u> has tarried home awhile? Brian

When Summer's heat slows all our feet,
We stroll through flower meadows sweet.
Who are they take snaps to capture
Scenes which give us all such rapture? Rosalie

When Autumn woods with russet glow,
Some note the bushes hung with sloe!
Who are they will add the gin
And bring the hip-flask with it in?   Brenda

When Winter wind whips leaves asunder
Or sparkling frost fills eyes with wonder,
Who t'is lingers in the chill
To answer mobile's urgent trill?   Alan

When valleys deep and hillsides steep
Make some folks breathless, some to creep,

Who are they can talk and climb?
There's one who has a friend sublime.
　　Pocket-sized, smart dial …
　Shared features? … His mobile?　　Alan

And who is it thinks she's a poet?!
She isn't! But she doesn't know it.
Just humour her and try to smile,
She may believe your harmless guile!　Rosalie

Alan, you win the award for the Backmarker with the most mobile style. (May your Mobile never be "sausage and mashed"! Cockney slang?)

For Keith's 80th Birthday

A man with a purpose,
He walks hill and dale
And follows his nose
To that pint of ale –
Over bridge and stream
And rickety stile,
To greet his Ice cream
With a beneficent smile.

Keith, a scholarly man
And very well read,
But Elizabeth would ban
Some things he has said!
Keith. You're four score – and more.
A wry wit – to the core.
And we all hope to tread
Where you have just lead
Greetings! Keith.

Sonia's 60th Birthday

Our lives have interwoven to such a degree
That you are ever in my memory
As a friend of the highest category.

We have shared holidays upon the ocean,
Where the ever constant motion
Made you and Ronnie have the notion
That for nausea one needs a potion,
Or all the fish will make 'commotion!'

To all your friends and family
Your gifts of love and serenity,
Support and wise diplomacy,
You have given so generously.

To My Good Friend Sue

Your fiftieth year brought activities new,
Retirement from work we know you'll not rue.
A rock and roll on the waves you pursue,
O'er forest and heath your horse's hooves flew,
Swum lengths of the pool with strength anew.

Now to Germany large with sister to view.
A launch into space? Just give us the cue!
Ready to glide over horizons new,
Where Tammy will sit, I haven't a clue.
This rhyme and a dinner I had to brew
To give you your due, our adventurous Sue.

(Tammy is Sue's dog)

To Sue - 1997

Off again to Chandlers Ford?
Well, Peter's there, you won't be bored.
Off again to Hailsham town?
Well, family love entwines you round.
Off again to help at Chailey?
Well, this duty makes you happy.
Off again to swim a mile??
Well, this is when I get your smile!

In Memory of Mick - Sep 2008

Mick, we will remember you
As kind and unassuming,
Quiet, firm and calming.
On our walks – just strolling.
At the pub – just telling
Stories with droll endings
In a voice like growling
And your face not showing
The way your wit is going.
And after a meal too filling,
You, like a bear, just snoozing!
Mick, ever kind and unassuming,
We will remember you.

To Flora – The Ladies who Sew

There are some ladies who sew,
With their needles they like to create.
They sit at a table and are very able
To quilt, applique and knit pretty cable –
But when Rosalie arrives very late,
They are scoffing Flora's scones from a plate,
Conversation is flowing, the scones are fast going
Down the throats of the ladies who sew
And loud peels of laughter rise through the rafters
To Brian who is up to – who knows?!

There's a hospitable lady we know,
Who encouraged her friend's creativity,
Their enthusiasm she fired
And their work was inspired –
But **one** gave her vibes of negativity!
As a challenge she did throw a lump of play-dough,
Plop! On the table, "Now see if you're able!"
And Margaret was hooked while Rosalie just looked
As a figure began to grow!
They all cried, "Well done,
We're having such fun!"
BUT will Rosalie get going – who knows?

For Stephanie's Sixtieth Birthday

Happy birthday dear Stephanie
You have reached maturity.
Forty and fifty are history
So "Zimmer" forward with dignity
Life really begins at sixty!

Joints may get stiff and creaky
And a certain loss of memory
You discover is **not** temporary,
Still Enjoy, Enjoy your maturity
Life really begins at Sixty – trust me – I'm a Septogenarian!

A Day with Eileen

What sunny days we've had Eileen,
In glorious gardens, we have seen
The Acers, in roseate hues a-gleaming,
Beside the lily lake a-dreaming
We stood and shared delight.
Later we viewed an unusual sight.
We sought the gardener, and so polite,

said, "Oh gardener, there on your mowing machine,
Such an exciting thing we've seen,
A sight which filled us with delight!
It was gambolling on the bank so green,
Lithe and black. Could it have been
An otter rare by the lake serene?"

"No, dear ladies what you might think
As so cute and lithe, was a vicious mink!"

Our 56th Anniversary - 2009

Dearest sweetheart, how could I know
When I met you so long ago,
At eighty you'd still be my beau
With plenty of yeast still in your dough!

You're the finest claret from a famed chateau;
You're my steady oak when strong winds blow;
But you come from a planet I'll never know
With a boyish humour that's Whacky-O!
You snooze and you snore and I love you so!

Now over the hill together we go,
Holding hands – please never let go,
As Time flows like a river to the wide unknown.
Go slow Time, slow the flow of the life we've known.

Jean's 60th Birthday - 1992

It was in Trinidad we met so long ago,
Time like the heaving sea, too swiftly does it flow.
Thirty or more years have tossed us to and fro,
But still we keep friendship's steady flame aglow.

Now at sixty, with many reefs explored,
Many ventures floated, your spirit we applaud.
To aspire to Senior Citizenship, the accolade you've scored.
With all the cut-price bargains, you never should be bored!
Welcome to this club elite we say with one accord.
For Ronnie and I to agree, should never be deplored.

Celebrating our family visit to Belgium after 50 years of friendship- 1996!

1946 – Rosalie greeted Sanki
With an English cup of tea,
When Sanki came to see
An English family.
And in July it will be
The anniversary –
Can you guess how many?
Well, now it is - fifty!

1947 – Sanki greeted Rosalie
With some Belgian quality
Chocolates (unknown) and sweets for me,
When I stayed with her family
In a cottage by the sea.
Oh, what hospitality!
It will be the anniversary
In July next year. Yes, fifty!

It has been our happy destiny
That our male progeny
Made bonds so brotherly,
Continuing friendship properly
To their very own progeny,
Exchanging visits annually
Into the future indefinitely
Well, perhaps another fifty!

To Tamsin on her 12th Birthday - Aug '95

There was a young girl called Tamsin
Who swam like a fish, sans fin!
She awoke one morn
And said with a yawn,
"Twelve years have gone
Since the day I was born,
I'll shout and I'll sing
And play the violin."
Which she did , and made quite a din!
That saucy young girl called Tamsin,
We pity her kith and her kin!

For Kali

I have just heard
From a diminutive bird,
A fact so absurd
I at once demurred,
"Kali is 40 on Tuesday", it said!

In my thoughts it occurred
That it's mind must be blurred,
I said, "Absurd bird",
It was not deterred.
"Kali is 40 on Tuesday" it churred.

I had to concur,
Though I knew you'd prefer
I would disbelieve her.
So I said with much cheer
"Life starts at 40", I purred.

Dianne

We had some tea
In the "Nutmeg Tree"
You and I.
We had a lot of chat
Knew where we were at,
You and I.

We had a lot of wine
As we sat down to dine,
You and I.
We had a lot of play
With Oliver that day
You and I.

We had a lot of food
And "cooed" at my "Dood"
You and I
We have had a lot of years,
Some laughter, some tears,
You and I.

('Dood' was the pet name for our dog.)

A Pearl Wedding and Three Birthdays - May 1994

Pensions, pearls and number thirty,
We gather here to celebrate.
The connecting links are somewhat quirky,
But whose is the important date?

We hope, Ann, today is "as happy as Larry",
This saying is apt, at any rate.
Thirty years since their decision to marry
And they're still together in wedded state.
Did Larry or Ann know their awful fate
When one of them landed on the other's plate?

At least they managed to collaborate
To produce a fine son – a daughter fair,
Whose return from China we had to await
For OAPS Ann and Larry, VSO Claire
With Ronnie and Rosalie their celebrations to share.
(Tongue in cheek!)

Tamsin and Lindsay
Neighbour's daughters.

Here come Tamsin and Lindsay,
Two charming creative pests.
Here come Lindsay and Tamsin,
Are we cursed or are we blessed?
Here come Tamsin and Lindsay
To come and disrupt our nest,
Here they come, there is no rest!
Tamsin has a smile of secret wickedness,
Lindsay's open smile belies her sauciness.
Watch out, watch out! The girls are about!

Crispin

Crispin is grandson number three
A bright and cheerful chap is he,
With eyes the blue of a summer sky
And hair so curly, I wonder why.
His smile so saucy will always endear,
His deep brown voice a joy to hear,
A natural charm, he's never shy.
Oh my, Oh my, it makes me sigh –
Seven years have now passed by.
Oh why, Oh why does time so fly?

Frey is grandson premier.
From the time of birth he was very dear
Because I was privileged to be right there.
As he would not always be near –
And some may think this very queer –
My maternal need for a pet became clear.
So Kushti came, shared life with us here.

("Kushti" or "Doody", our beloved lurcher)

To Nicholas on his 35th Birthday - June '92

In Trinidad where the sun is incessant
Thirty-five years ago
The birth of a boy so innocent
Such happiness did bestow
Upon us, his parents, it was apparent
That he was the best, you know!

In Yorkshire where the sun is inconstant,
Now thirty-five years have flown.
The birth of two boys makes him a parent
And wisdom and love have grown.
Now we heartily hope for a job, heaven sent,
He deserves the best, ever known.

Now up to the Lakes where mountains ascend
For a holiday break you drive
With Jean-F and sons who'll make it so pleasant.
The sun and the scenery will all contrive
To make your stay such a wonderful blend
You will hope it will never end.

Fond Farewell to Ivan and Family - Oct '94

To Ivan, our dear son, taking on a challenge new,
The promise of the Golden West where money does accrue.
Golden sun, golden sand,
Golden lentils in your stew!
A honeyed life for a Golden "Pooh",
For which I know you have a taste.
So to your future now make haste.

For all of the family, it is the end of an era
During which we shared our time, growing ever closer and dearer.
Now golden sun, and golden honey draw you ever nearer,
Promise of climate with no peer
For which you knew it made much sense
To trade in dollars instead of pence!

So Ivan dear and family,
This parting we'll endure
For the fulfilment of your dreams, your ability will ensure.
Golden sun, golden sand and golden air so pure.
On Alex's "wheeze" make golden cure,
For which I know we all desire.
For you, more hours to play, less work to tire.

Dear Ivan, our loving prayer is that your true endeavour
For the health and joy of your family will reap success forever.
Not Golden taps on Golden baths, but Gold contentment ever.
"Pooh" philosophy – who said he's not so clever?
For you our hearts will always yearn,
While awaiting your return.

(Ivan is a trader in honey - They returned 2000)

A Thank-You to Sue Watts - 1993
For helping me when I was struggling with a very old computer writing up our New Zealand holiday of 1992

Dear Sue, "thank you", a friend so true,
With your skill consummate
My lines you pursue
A readable story to create,
All because I haven't a clue
How to begin to "process" as you do!
Dear Sue, "thank you, you're almost through,
Your own needs sublimated,
But the end is in view,
With reading you're satiated,
Your "Family History" you can now do
And "processing" knowledge I can accrue.
Dear Sue, "thank you", I'll start anew.
Now letters, photos all collated
The narrative finished, not much to do.
It matters not 'tis belated,
Just as long as 'tis created
For the family to construe.
The knowledge lost - if not for you!

Sue W, Again April - 1995
With apologies to Edward Lear!

There was a young lady of Pett,
Who had an amusing wit.
She had a few hens,
And wrote with quill pens,
That charming young lady from Pett.

There was a young lady of Fairlight,
She was incredibly bright,
She "did herself in"
With too much gardenin'
Which put her friends in a plight.

There was a young lady of Guestling,
For her garden, she "had a real thing".
She said, "I'm damned if I let
These weeds ever get
To root in my plot in Guestling." God wot!

There was a young lady whose worth
Was far more than the plants in the earth.
To her kith and her kin
She cried, "It's a sin
For my flowers to suffer a dearth".

There was a young lady whose lower limb
Caused her much pain and suffering.
To rest she was opposed,
Cried, "Devil take the hindmost!"
So they amputated the offending limb!

(Not really!)

There was a young lady whose leg
Had become just a wooden peg.
Her friends said, "Ho, Ho,
We told you so,"
To the foolish young lady "sans" leg!

That conscientious lady of Pett,
The garden she must try to forget.
Rest leg and write rhymes,
See friends, have good times.
The leg, it will heal, just don't fret.

There was a young lady of Fairlight
Whose husband came to her plight.
She said, "Pull that weed
Before it can seed."
A decade on she left her plot in Fairlight.

<u>To Ronnie – His 63rd Birthday - 1992</u>

Forty-five years have passed away
Since *"sitting in the sea one day*
Who did I see not far away,
But a fair-haired Tarzan boy
Wading towards me – Oh so coy"!

Now your hairs are hard to see,
But you will never need to plea –
"Will you still need me, will you still feed me
Now I'm sixty-three?"

Because you are so precious to me,
Your enduring love, your humour and glee,
Everlasting traits, which are the key
To your loveable personality.
(P.S. You've found yet another ability - With D.I.Y. you seem to agree!!
but not for long!!)

Flora's Birthday - August 3rd 2009

Flora Dora, our Power Flower,
How does your garden grow,
With peppers, beans and aubergines
And sweet corn all in a row.

Flora Dora, Flower Power,
Busy each and every hour.
Are you a bee or are you a flower?
Each are at home in a flower bower.

One a 'doer' with a lot of buzz,
The other observes what the world does.
So Flora Flower "beehive" in your bower,
Make your days sweet and never sour!

Loves Labour Won - April 2015
To My Dear Friend Flora

Flora Dora had a plan.
A dream, a scheme
A flight of fancy.
She fell in love with
A hunk … not a man,
But a chunky, dunky red van!!
With a place to eat,
And a place to sleep,
It also has a very nice "beep"!
It has shelves to locate
All your cups and your plates.
And it even has room for a party!
There is space for the dog,
But where is the 'bog'?
If you feel the need to be 'farty'!

Nigel
(An airline pilot who loved to sail and paint pictures)

You have not gone –
You are in the wind as the sail billows,
You are in the frothy wake.
You are in your garden flowers and in the green willows.
You are there.

Above the lark's flight,
Where the clouds carpet the sky
You still fly. You fly.

In the colours of your paints
Always in our sight,
You are there.

Even the syrup of the crepes
And frosted glass rim on a Marguerite
Bring back memories, happy, sharp and sweet.
We may sigh. We may cry.

Do we ever hear, "When push comes to shove"
We smile. We know you have not gone,
You are in its familiarity
You are there. You are there.

Your love of life and family
Is how we remember you with love
And will always be your legacy.
When a son or daughter laughs or a grandchild achieves,
You are there in memory,
You are there.

Sonia & Nigel's Golden Anniversary - 12th June 2004

It's such a pity
    This is not witty
        But this ditty
            Is just a bitty
                About a pretty
                    Girl and a gritty
                        Guy ...

A dashing young pilot was he
And she worked for BOAC.
Her dark eyes set him aflame,
He said, "I'll date that young dame".
His good looks she couldn't ignore,
So they married in June '54.

Then he whisked her away
For fifty years and a day
To a land far over the sea –
The exotic isles of the Caribee –
And quite soon the twosome were three!

Baby David had a strange yellow hue,
Which colour he soon outgrew.
No Chinese involved – Nigel knew!
Then Richard arrived two years later –
Such a tease to his lovely young mater.

At a kid's party, (much hullabaloo!)
We met. Rick and Nick were just two.
The Heath's life was fulsome and fast,
Eight years elapsed, but at last
A baby was born for them all to adore.
But now there are granddaughters, more and more!

Ceylan, Carissa, Jessica and Josie,
Green-eyed Laura and cute little Sophie,
Grandsons Jeremy, James and Robert
Keep Sonia and Nigel awake and alert!
Preventing a snooze is no mean feat –
Prod, prod, nod, nod – asleep in their seats.

Now a much loved Gran is she,
And equally lovable is he.
Her eyes are not quite the same
But he's a special date with his dame
Which none of us will ignore,
Their Golden in 2004.

Time has whisked away,
Fifty years and a day
Since they wed and left "Blighty"
For an isle in the Carabee.
Happy anniversary ….   *Enjoy* .. with your family.

To Pat

Twinkle, twinkle starlet Pat,
How I wonder what you're at!
Do you leap and stretch so high
To reach the Jumbos in the sky?

Twinkle, twinkle, you're a star.
Husband Brian made your car!
Cause enough to make you cry,
But now you're glad when you speed by.

Twinkle, twinkle Birthday Pat
Five decades is what you're at!
Now half a century has gone by
Like a twinkling of an eye.
Enjoy the next half century!

Apologies to Lewis Carroll - 1980s to 1990s

"You're getting old Mother dear", the young man said,
"And your hair has become quite white,
And yet you incessantly run round a field,
Do you think, at your age, it is right?"

"In my youth," the Mother replied to her son,
"I feared it might shake up the brain,
But now that I'm perfectly sure I have none,
Why, I do it again and again."

"You're getting old," said the youth, "as I mentioned before,
And years you have two score and more,
And yet you continue to ride through the wood,
Do you think at your age, that you should?"

"In my youth," said his mater as she shook her grey hair,
I kept all my limbs very supple,
By riding, and swimming and diving with air,
I have memories, more than a couple."

"You're getting old, Mother dear," the youth said with a wink,
"And your skin has wrinkles, I think,
Yet you often wear shorts which show your thighs,
Do you think at your age that is wise?"

"In my youth," she sighed, "we lived in the heat,
And shorts were the common attire,
But the habit dies hard to strip near complete
When the sun shines hot as a fire."

"You're getting old, Mother dear," he said turning pale,
"And you look uncommonly frail,
And yet you took flight on a parakite,
Do you think, at your age, that is right?"

"In my youth," she replied, with a smile on her face,
I frequently envied the birds,
'78 in Corfu was the time and the place;
'Make hay in the sun' – so I've heard."

"You're old Mother dear, and your hair is quite white,
And grandsons you have quite a few.
It is time to quit the exercise bike,
Stay home and cook us a stew."

"Be off, " she said, "Or I'll tan your backside"
As she shovelled up shit from the shires,
"Your Father and I, White Water have tried,
Adventure in life is now all we require."
(Comment – premature ageism now in 2018!)

Suzie's 30th Birthday - May '92

Twelve plus years ago, for sure, we met you first, a girl so pure!
Now quietly confident, kind, mature, may golden bloom life's prime endure.
May fruitful challenges still hold allure.

Thirty years have hastened past. At M&S you climbed so fast
A butterfly your chrysalis cast – emerged a systems analyst at last
For Laura Ashley – all were outclassed.

Our son has helped you to complete, creation of a boy so neat
That all who see say, "What a feat!"
His looks and brains cannot be beat! "Create another", we all entreat.
Break the rules, they are for fools – we want some girls, they are such pearls!

A Bit of Blarney for Barnie the Belle of the Ball – 1984

Now …	Crowborough is a little town of small renown,
	Whose only claim to fame
	Is the lovely forest of Ashdown.
But …	In this town of small renown
	There lives a shapely dame,
Who …	Despite great limits on her time
	Has energy sublime,
And …	With voice and tape, licks into shape
	A troupe of "Liquorice Allsorts",
Whom …	With voice of thunder she exhorts …
	"Discipline your body
	We shall be vigorous – not ploddy."

    Bouncing bosoms, flailing thighs,
    All limbs in disarray,
    Still we leap, and spring so high;
    Our willing lot is to obey.
    Bending and twisting like corkscrews
    Has made our motley crew,
    Her Wednesday, Thursday eager "Gells",
    Into the Barnies Belles.

Now …	Crowborough is a little town of small renown,
	Whose second claim to fame
	Is the lithe, lissom, lively dame
	Who made her classes such a game,
Her …	"Discipline your body" refrain
	Has become the universal aim.
Now …	Tonight we hold our glasses in a toast
	To "Barnie" who gave her classes the most.
	We'll give "reach and twist and bend" a rest
	While we laugh and eat and drink at The Crest.

Another bit of Blarney for Barnie The Belle of the Ball – 1985

Thanks to Barnie it's come to pass
The yuletide gathering of our class
Descends upon the Crest en masse.
Its hapless guests begin to cringe
For Barnie's belles are on the binge.

They're lithe and fit and full of strength,
Ready to eat and drink at length –
Out of the window goes Barnie's motto,
Under the table some may fall blotto!

To Barnie we drink a fulsome toast,
Our "disciplined bodies" are her boast.
Thanks for making pain <u>such</u> fun –
A second year of torture done.

But really Barnie you are such a dear,
And as I said in rhyme last year,
Disciplining bodies" is your forté,
But underneath you're really naughty!

So, Margaret, love and best wishes from all here,
We would like to express with a hearty cheer!
Thanks once again from all the fair, fat and forty,
All those slim, trim and twenty,
All those plump or thin and thirty,
All those slow or nifty and fifty,
And have we some steady, sweet and sixty?

To Irene 1980s

Dear Friend, please excuse – A pitiful dittyful
    Rhyme without time
    The verse gets worse
    And the meter does peter …
    To an odious ode –
    But now I have done it
    Can you bear to con it
    A salute in a sonnet!

The Cottage – "Rosemary" and Irene
    Lived with each other
    And grew together.
    Three years were shared,
    Hours, moments, friends who cared,
    Tea, toast and sympathy …
    And "is there honey still for tea?" (Well, it rhymes!)

    There were weeks they lived leanly,
    Some evenings were lonely,
    But could Irene
    Who lived life so keenly
    Be long on her own -
    Not with a phone!

    With hair so bouncy
    And voice so brown,
    Manner so sprightly,
    A 'girl' about town.

    Then along came Harry,
    A voice from the past,
    And he would not tarry
    He knew love would last
    So Spring-time they marry,
    Rebirth of love, hope and joie de vivre
Dear friend, we wish you when you leave …..
    But Harry put a meter on your phone
    Or rush out and get a loan!

Holidays at Triton   For Marvin

July 1996

    Last summer's holidays are far away,
    But do you remember the happy day
    We spent cycling along the Cuckoo trail?
    Another day you took the kite for a sail,
    It twisted and turned and hit the earth.
    It gave us trouble but caused you mirth!

    To Brighton to see some Dinosaurs,
    Some had claws just like hacksaws.
    Later, on the promenade by the sea
    We saw some people from ITV.
    You wanted to get on the Lottery Show,
    So on to the carousel you had to go,
    But you never saw your claim to fame,
    It was all cut out. Oh what a shame!

August 1996

    Your cousins you joined, now three boys –
    (I am now going to change the kind of verse).
    You were all very happy and made more noise,
    And your eating habits got worse and worse!
    In windy sunshine, sea at low-tide,
    You ran on the sands and looked in the rocks,
    Into some mud you managed to slide.
    What a black mess in your shoes and your socks!

    Duffy, Meg, Kushti and all of you,
    Climbed a steep hill with a great view.
    Then home to Crowborough for two nights.
    You all went with grandad to fly the kite.
    Crispin had no turn, neither did Frey,
    And that was nearly the end of your stay.
    What a wonderful, sunny holiday.

Then by train we went to Harrogate,
You came too for Frey's 10th birthday date.
The cave at How Stean Gorge you voted as "great".
Frey's friend came too, and you had such fun.
But now your holidays are nearly done.
So we caught the fast train from Harrogate,
And home you went for your school-term date

Holiday on the Sands 1996
Marvin, Frey, Rosalie, Crispin and Kushti

Christmas 1996

Summer's long gone and now Christmas has too.
NickyKaliFreyCrispinMarvinOliverAlexIvanandSue,
At Triton all stayed – and Great Uncle David and all,
Great Uncle David and all.

They chatted and played and stayed up late,
Christmas presents the better to anticipate,
And lots of new toys and all,
Lots of new toys and all.

After Christmas their next visit was in store,
Such joy to see when we opened the door.
Oliver remembered Kushti's front paw
Had been bandaged and booted because it was sore –
Now gone bandage, boot and all,
Gone bandage, boot and all.

Our dear grandsons all share one common core,
That is our "Dood" whom they all adore.
They smother and cuddle her all on the floor,
They feed her their crusts when her eyes implore,
They stroke her and pat her and hold her paw,
They give her crisps when she asks for more,
Frey, Crispin, Marvin and all,
Oliver, Alex, Marvin and all.

Next, the snow lay all around, and it blew and flew.
The Case-Lengs and Marvin went sledging – it's true.
We celebrated Marvin's birthday, but missing a few,
Because Jeremy did not come – the reason we knew,
And Suzie, Oliver and Alex were in bed with the flu,
Her Mother, Father and all, Mother, Father and all.

The boys played in the snow, what a soggy crew!
Their clothes in the drier, Nana constantly threw.
Marvin's one pair of shoes got more than its due.
Grandad had a cold and everyone knew!
Oh, what fun we had, one and all,
What fun we had, one and all.

We sat down to meals and ate food galore,
Nana cooked many eggs, but Frey, Marvin called
                                    "More",
Nana said "The grandsons I adore are becoming a bore,
To ask for more should be forbidden by law,
No bacon, eggs, cheese at all,
No more for you at all!

So when Grandad's in a spin, Nana's in a stew,
And the boys are in a pickle, now this is the cue
For Nicky or Kali to put another pot to brew,
But so many cups of tea make me run to the loo.
Bloated, tired are we all.
But now I so miss you and all.

The Leng Family in 1993.
Susie, Rosalie, Ronnie, Kali,
Nick, Jeremy, Ivan,
Frey, Marvin, Alex,
Kushti, Crispin, Oliver